ENDORSEMENTS

One of the reasons I love *The Scribe* is because not only does it teach you about dreams, but it actually helps you in the process of remembering your dreams. We are entering a season when the Lord is restoring the power of the night watch in the Church. We will be arising and praying as well as sleeping and receiving! I believe James has created a tool that will be used from one generation to another generation as each wields the sword of revelation to build the Church for the future and unlock the Kingdom of God. *The Scribe* is an excellent source of experiential and practical principles that will assist you in learning to rule the night.

Chuck D. Pierce
President, Glory of Zion International, Inc.
Vice President, Global Harvest Ministries

Dr. James Goll knows the voice of the Holy Spirit as few men do. He has built a vast repertory from his expertise in the spirit realm. His knowledge of the areas of the prophetic, dream interpretation, and intimacy with God in prayer propelled him to develop *The Scribe* as a wonderful tool to enable us to record our devotion times and visions in a constructive, detailed way.

Dr. Barbie L. Breathitt
Author of *Dream Encounters,*
Gateway to the Seer Realm, and *Dream Seer*

James Goll has blessed us with vital truths and living examples to understand and fulfill dreams. The reader will discover the real purpose and meaning of dreams. Biblical and practical guidelines are given to help any individual discern whether the dream was divinely given and how to properly apply its meaning. *The Scribe* is another wonderful tool. James, thanks for helping us understand and fulfill our spiritual dreams.

Dr. Bill Hamon
Apostle, Bishop of Christian International Ministries Network

The Scribe, as with *The Prophet,* by Dr. James Goll is a timely and valuable contribution to the church of our generation. We are living in an era when God is truly raising up a great company of His prophets to impact the world with a mighty infusion and invasion of His Kingdom and righteousness. Many might ask questions, such as: what is the difference between being prophetic and being a prophet? Can any believer be a prophet? What qualifies a prophet? Who are the prophets? Can I serve as a prophet? This book answers those questions and more and will stir hunger in you to embrace the heart and will of God for this hour.

Dr. Patricia King
Founder, Patricia King Ministries

Francis Bacon said, "Reading maketh a full man; speaking, a ready man; writing, an exact man." After reading James' *The Scribe,* I would add, "and dreaming, a complete man." Those dreams I once dismissed now have meaning, and I have the prophetic guide, James Goll, to thank. For God speaks in the language of image, symbol, color, and sense, and nobody does a better job of explaining the prophetic realm and its language than James Goll.

Dr. Lance Wallnau
Lance Learning Group

If we are to interpret the signs and the times, then we need master technicians to help us. It has been my great pleasure to know and work with

James Goll over the years. I cannot think of anyone more spiritually prepared or experienced in the pragmatics of God's revelatory ways than this man. I have heard him teach on intrinsic and extrinsic dreams in particular—brilliant! That alone is worth the price of *The Scribe*. This is the material that will put wings under the feet of the process that you need to move quickly into that new land of the Spirit that awaits.

Graham Cooke
Founder, Brilliant Perspectives
Brilliant Book House

James Goll is a friend and a respected father in the prophetic movement. The message in *The Scribe* is one of the best I have read. It is full of wisdom, anointing, and presence of the Holy Spirit. Once I began to read it, I could not put it down. Within these pages you will encounter a stirred desire to know and hear the voice of the Lord while being activated through the wisdom and instruction of how to prophesy. *"But I desire even more that you impart prophetic revelation to others. Greater gain comes through the one who prophesies"* (1 Corinthians 14:5 The Passion Translation). It is my belief that all who read this book will grow in wisdom and anointing to hear and release the prophetic word of the Lord and that *The Scribe* will become a classic message for years to come. Thank you, James, for this timely word.

Rebecca Greenwood
President and Cofounder Christian Harvest International Strategic Prayer Apostolic Network
Author of *Authority to Tread, Let Our Children Go, Defeating Strongholds of the Mind, Glory Warfare*

For every believer who desires to comprehend the Spirit language of God, *The Scribe* is an invaluable resource. Dr. James Goll, a prophetic papa in the modern prophetic movement, is graced with a "scribal anointing" and an Issachar prophetic forecast to assist us in stewarding and interpreting the secrets of God through dreams, prophetic words, revelation knowledge, and personal God encounters. This well-written, step-by-step interactive study guide and journal will equip every believer with the keys of impartation and information needed to become one of God's trusted interpreters of the things of the Spirit. I fully endorse and recommend *The Scribe* for those who are ready.

Dr. Hakeem Collins
Prophetic Voice, Author, International Speaker
Author *Heaven Declares, Prophetic Breakthrough, Command Your Healing, 101 Prophetic Ways God Speaks*

Journaling is one of the most practical and overlooked ways to daily encounter with God. He's always speaking, it's just often that we aren't listening. I love how James Goll's *The Scribe* breaks down different ways to journal, and discern what God is saying during the day and even prophetically in the night while we dream. As you plug into the source, be still and ready to listen, be prepared to fill your journal with deeper encounters and revelations with God. He is always pursuing us!

Ana Werner
Founder of Ana Werner Ministries
President, Eagles Network
Author of *The Seer's Path, Seeing Behind the Veil, The Warrior's Dance*,
Coauthor of *Accessing the Greater Glory*
www.anawerner.org

I have known Papa James Goll for years. His wisdom, grace, and big heart are such a blessing to the Body of Christ. As a time of awakening is upon us, the Lord is bringing His Church back to the disciplines. James' book *The Scribe* explores a discipline that can at times be overlooked, especially if we hold to an attitude of being too busy. The discipline of journaling our journey is good for the soul and the spirit, both for ourselves and for the generations to come. The saints of old chronicled their journey and testimony, reminding us and encouraging us about the goodness of God! As you read this book, *The Scribe,* you will be awakened to journal the revelation of the whispers of God. You will be invited to record the dream downloads from heaven, now to be retained for a lifetime and for those who will follow! Writing the revelation down helps us celebrate answers to prayer and remind us of how God came through!

Steven and Rene Springer
International Speakers
Co-Founders Global Presence Ministries
Apostolic Overseers, Global Presence Leaders Alliance

I've always journaled my night dreams often to discover their accuracy years after I had them. If I hadn't journaled them, I would have forgotten them and missed God's voice of hope in difficult seasons. I journal prayer points, applicable promises to my problems, and plan my day and write my goals using my journal. I've never considered that someone would write such an inspiring book about writing things down. James Goll's, *The Scribe,* is both a spiritual and relational journey over words as well as a practical one. He will inspire you to "write it down" and when you do, you'll awaken to a growing encounter with the Holy Spirit over *words.* This book will impact you.

Jennifer Eivaz
Executive Pastor, Harvest Church Turlock California
Founder, Harvest Ministries International
Author of *Prophetic Secrets* and *Glory Carriers*

THE
SCRIBE

JAMES W. GOLL

THE
SCR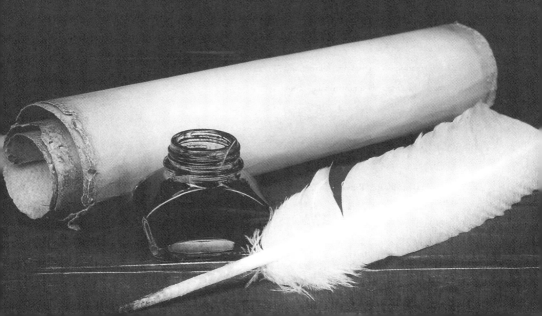BE

RECEIVING AND RETAINING
REVELATION THROUGH
JOURNALING

DESTINY IMAGE® PUBLISHERS, INC.
P.O. Box 310, Shippensburg, PA 17257-0310
"Promoting Inspired Lives."

This book and all other Destiny Image and Destiny Image Fiction books are available at Christian bookstores and distributors worldwide.

Cover design by Eileen Rockwell

For more information on foreign distributors, call 717-532-3040.

Reach us on the Internet: www.destinyimage.com.

ISBN 13 TP: 978-0-7684-5048-4

ISBN 13 eBook: 978-0-7684-5049-1

ISBN 13 HC: 978-0-7684-5051-4

ISBN 13 LP: 978-0-7684-5050-7

For Worldwide Distribution, Printed in the U.S.A.

1 2 3 4 5 6 7 8 / 24 23 22 21 20

DEDICATION

With gratefulness, I dedicate this book, *The Scribe,* to our Lord Jesus Christ, the Dream Come True! Jesus is the Scribe. Jesus is the Word made manifest. Jesus is the Prophet! Jesus is our Teacher. Jesus is our Shepherd. Jesus is the One who brings Good News! Jesus the Chief Apostle of our faith. Jesus is the Savior. Jesus is our Healer. JESUS IS LORD!

With a heart that overflows with the pen of the ready writer, I compose my prose unto Jesus our King! Indeed, only Jesus is the King of kings!

ACKNOWLEDGMENTS

Every work is a team effort. Every effective tool becomes a composite of the strengths of several, and yet God uses the voice of a few to bring the message to the many. So it is with *The Scribe*. With this in mind, in a culture of honor, I express some tokens of acknowledgments to a few.

I am grateful for my relationship with Destiny Image Publishers over the years. *The Scribe* becomes a stand-alone work, and yet an amazing complement to the three major prophetic works I have composed with Destiny Image over the decades: *The Seer, Dream Language* and *The Prophet*. So first I say "Thank You" to all of the leadership of Destiny Image from over the many years. You were the first publishing company to take a risk on a relatively unknown praying prophet with my first book, *The Lost Art of Intercession*. So thanks goes to the publishing house, staff, and leadership of Destiny Image/Nori Media Group.

Also, I always want to give gratitude to the staff, board, advisers, and partners of God Encounters Ministries. Again, *The Scribe,* contains new material and yet includes excerpts of years of collaboration and cooperative efforts. I regularly thank the Lord for the honor and privilege of walking with a cast of characters who walk in the character of Jesus. Thank you!

I want to thank the readers, too. You are my audience. You have given me a measure of your trust, time, and investment. So I want to honor and acknowledge the thousands and even millions of followers of Jesus who have tuned their ear my way to listen to my voice over the past forty-five-plus years of full-time vocational ministry.

Thank you to each and every one!
Dr. James W. Goll

My heart overflows with a good theme; I address my verses to the King; my tongue is the pen of a ready writer.

PSALM 45:1

CONTENTS

YOUR JOURNEY INTO JOURNALING

I extend to you a personal invitation into the ancient pathways of being a scribe. Journaling is a strategic tool that has been used throughout the generations as a means of capturing and retaining special moments, special thoughts, special prayers, and special revelations in a personal manner.

Journaling is not a boring task. Oh no! Journaling is full of adventure and life. It has at least three different expressions: 1) Devotional; 2) Revelatory; and 3) Historical. So whether journaling is used to increase your personal devotional life with God or used as a tool to retain dreams and visions or recording lessons from life, each style and format is very important.

I divided this book into *seven distinct sections,* each with a specific purpose. Section One grants an inspiring vision of why *The Scribe* was written and its purpose. Section Two contains seven lessons with Keys for the Journey. Section Three builds on the journey with seven more lessons on Handling Revelatory Realms, while Section Four rounds out our short essays with seven additional lessons on Growing in Stewardship. Now that is a lot of practical wisdom right there!

Then we move on into our personal journey with the opportunity to apply what you have learned. Yes, Section Five is My Personal Journal. Now put feet to your encounters with the Holy Spirit and do it! Just do it! I give you practical how-to models laid out just for you filled with inspirational insights to encourage you along the way.

Then we round the corner into the last two sections of the book that are also critically important for completing your new adventure. Section Six is an abbreviated Glossary of Terms, and Section Seven provides a list of Recommended Reading titles.

So, *The Scribe* gives you the entire alphabet from A to Z in the world of journaling.

I trust that you will have many special moments recorded, retained, interpreted, and ready to share with others in your Journey into Journaling!

Blessings!

James W. Goll
God Encounters Ministries
Goll Ideation LLC

SECTION ONE

ENCOUNTERING GOD THROUGH JOURNALING

Receiving Revelation by Journaling

My heart overflows with a good theme; I address my verses to the King; my tongue is the pen of a ready writer.

PSALM 45:1

The theme verse for this entire book is Psalm 45:1. I absolutely love this verse. Before the psalmist goes into a task or a calling or an anointing, he talks about the heart— ***"My heart overflows** with a good theme."* Then, *"I address my verses to the King; my tongue is the pen of a ready writer."* Let me give a little understanding on this verse.

Matthew 12:34 and Luke 6:45 state that *"out of the abundance of the heart the mouth speaks"* (NKJV). I believe that out of the abundance of God's heart, His mouth speaks too. Communication, prayer, and communion with God, is not a one-way street. Believers have a personal and a relational exchange with their heavenly Father. What goes up, comes back down. What comes down, goes back up. It is a relationship—not a give and take, but a give and receive bond of love.

Some people look at journaling as a dry, stodgy, old, studious discipline. But years ago when I was discussing one of my books, I said, "By the way, this is a contemporary read about the spiritual disciplines." Then, while I was still talking, the Holy Spirit interrupted me and said, "By the way, these are not as much spiritual disciplines as they are spiritual *privileges.*"

So, I ask you to come to this subject of journaling with fresh eyes, open ears, and a welcoming heart. This is not as much about your discipline's capacity, although that's very important, as it is about the Lord's yearning and longing to communicate back and forth with His people.

"My heart overflows with a good theme..." Is your heart overflowing? When your heart is overflowing with God's goodness, it is looking for a place and a people to impact. God will give you an assignment, a theme—and when you fulfill that assignment, your heart will constantly rejoice in His presence.

"I address my verses to the King...." There are three dimensions of journaling: 1) devotional; revelatory; and historical. We will be examining each of these dimensions and you will discover that each one brings home the importance of addressing your verses, your life's moments with your Savior and King of kings.

"...my tongue is a pen of a ready writer." I pray that your spirit will awaken to the privilege of interchange and exchange with your heavenly Father through journaling—writing what's in your heart and receiving what's in His heart for you.

THE VISION

Do you have a clear vision of the purpose of journaling? I admit I slip in and out of that clear vision, but I try to keep focused on it. Without a vision you will lose perspective and your intimate relationship with God will become hazy. But when you have a clear-cut vision of why journaling is imperative, you will continue to bask in His glory daily.

Five purposes for journaling your life are:

1. To encounter God, which is the primary purpose.

2. To record and retain revelation received from God.

3. To aid you in attaining your prayer goals.

4. To document instructions and guidelines from God.

5. To provide a space and place to reflect and evaluate your life.

The primary purpose of journaling is to *encounter God*. Do you want to encounter God in a more intimate way? Journaling accomplishes that goal. I journal because I want to hear His voice, know His heart, and walk in His ways. And I believe you do too. If so, you might just say right now, "Amen, count me in." Great! I applaud your enthusiasm. So, having a clear vision of the purpose of journaling begins with acknowledging that you want to encounter God.

The second purpose of journaling is to *record and retain the revelations* He gives you—otherwise, it acts like runoff water. He provides living water of revelation but if you don't record it, it's like water that just runs off and away—it isn't captured in a receptacle having a channeled use.

The third purpose of journaling is as an *aid to your prayer life*. Journaling helps you keep track of your prayers and your goals. When a prayer is answered and you record it, you are providing proof positive that God hears your prayers and they are important to Him. You can also follow along with prayers that have been heard but may not be addressed because He is waiting for the right time—His perfect timing. Journaling gives you a way to express your feelings and frustrations so you and God can work on them together.

Number four's journal purpose is that it acts as a *place to document guidelines and instructions* God gives you to balance your life most successfully. Journaling is a place to record lessons you are learning as you travel along in life's journey.

The fifth reason to journal is that it *gives you a space and a place to reflect and evaluate* your life. I tend to be a contemplator, and contemplators, in particular, need time to process events and activities that they face; we search for a deeper spiritual life. Everyone needs to process things that happen to and around us—some react quickly, others strategize. Journaling invites God into your time of processing.

RETAINING AND STEWARDING REVELATION

Journaling is a tried and tested, natural and spiritual tool that assists you in recording life's lessons and aids you in discerning the voice of the Holy Spirit. Journaling is a fundamental and clearly used biblical tool.

By the way, don't get caught up in issues that journaling is writing new chapters of the Bible. No, that isn't this, nor is this "automatic handwriting" or anything of that nature. This journaling is from a heart overflowing with the free will of a relational exchange of God with you, you with God, and this might sound a little unusual—you with yourself.

Journaling is a fundamental and clearly used biblical tool to help us retain and then properly steward what the Holy Spirit speaks to us.

During my life journey, I have discovered at least three valid expressions, or dimensions, of journaling. Some people become a specialist of one type, but there are at least three valid and distinct expressions of journaling. There are multiple expressions of journaling, each with a distinct purpose and each with a different style.

Three Dimensions of Journaling

The first dimension, which most people are familiar with, is *devotional journaling* or dialoguing devotionally with God. The second, which is my expertise, is *revelatory journaling.* The third is *historical journaling,* which is documenting lessons from your life's journey.

Let's look at ***devotional journaling***. Devotional journaling has a lot to do with your Bible. It has a lot to do with your personal relationship with God. Devotional journaling creates a space to grow in deeper communion with God and allows fellowshipping with the Holy Spirit. This may mean praying in tongues and then to just start writing. You may end up writing an interpretation to what you just prayed, or it might be an answer to prayer. We speak mysteries to God in the spirit, and what might be coming back down might be an inspiration of an interpretation or it might be the Holy Spirit giving you answers to your prayer.

Another way of saying it is growing in greater intimacy with Christ. That is what Jeanne Guyon would have taught in her understandings on beholding the beauty of the Lord, and then writing it. This can get into a dimension almost of inspired poetry.[1]

A friend of mine went through a very dry spiritual spell, so he took the Book of Romans and prayed and then journaled what he received from God through the Book of Romans. So there's many approaches to journaling, especially devotional journaling.

Recently I had the delight of sitting with some friends who live in California. I was so surprised when my friend's wife brought out to the patio a stack of journals, about ten of them. It was so exciting to me because neither of them knew that I was actually researching this topic and getting ready to prepare a presentation.

She pointed to the journals and said to me, "This journal is my recorded prayers. This one is where I write my dreams. This journal is where I keep my life goals. This journal, get this, is where I am now recording what I eat." Journaling can have many valid and helpful purposes, including accountability—but remember this, it is a *privilege* not just a discipline. So, journaling is all about growing in greater intimacy with Christ. Whatever you call it, just do it.

This approach in journaling is used by many in their devotional walk with the Lord. Let's consider some of the classic books that have been written throughout the years that address this topic. A book I learned a lot from was written by my friends, Dr. Mark and Patty Virkler, *Communion with God*. By the way, I have the original manual they released. As I studied through it, the wisdom within helped superglue the pieces together that I already believed, completing the puzzle concerning communing with God.

If you're more into church history, I recommend reading *The Interior Castle* written by Saint Teresa of Avila, first published in 1588. It is still one of the most widely read classics. This book is a record of devotional and revelatory encounters where the Holy Spirit leads her through the Book of John, chapter 14 that says, *"In My Father's house are many mansions..."* (John 14:2)—the interior castle. And, we are the temple of God. When reading this book, oh how I found peace in the first room in the mansion, the second room in the mansion, the third room in the mansion.... I didn't know these places existed and I gave myself to it; it marked my life. Not only that, this book later impacted the life of my late wife, Michal Ann. She even dedicated a chapter to Teresa of Avila in her book, *A Call to the Secret Place*.

These people, as well as thousands more, have written books that touch people's hearts, minds, and spirits—most started as devotional journals of revealing their encounters with God. Maybe your writings will inspire your family, church, community, state, nation, and the world. This could be your expertise! Devotional journals are treasure chests. Writing your prayers, pausing, listening, and recording God's answers are the beginning of lives changed. We'll come back to that specific topic a little later.

Revelatory journaling is the tool for recording revelatory experiences. I have a lot of experience with this type of journaling. The prophet Daniel's revelatory encounters are revealed in the Book of Daniel 7:1 (NIV). If it's good enough for Daniel, it's good enough for today's believers as well: *"In the first year of Belshazzar king in Babylon, Daniel had a **dream, and visions** passed through his mind as he was lying in bed. **He wrote down** the substance of his dream."*

I remember when my wife went through nine straight weeks of heavenly visitation and she said, "I can't even keep up with all of this." We had to learn how to record what she was experiencing because each night was something different. These records became a treasure chest for us.

Your actual, physical journal might be a fancy, awesome, leather-bound booklet. My daughter, Rachel, made one like that for me. Or it might be a little spiral notebook, funky and weird, like one I have that says, "Go for It." This is one of my treasures because that's exactly what journaling can be—a just-do-it treasure chest of God encounters.

So what did Daniel do after he had his dream and visions? The Bible says, *"...then he wrote the dream down and related the following summary of it"* (Daniel 7:1). Don't necessarily get all caught up in all the minutia of the dream and/or vision, just see the big picture, write it down, and then always go for the main and the plain and the major subject being addressed.

Let's consider other relevant books highlighting our topic. Albert and Anna Rountree were a writing team and friends of mine for many years. Anna Rountree wrote a book titled *The Heavens Opened: Revealing a Fresh Vision of God's Love for You* and *The Priestly Bride: Revealing the Mystery of Our Betrothal to God*. Her first book, *The Heavens Opened,* is an amazing read! It's content comes from all the trances and visions that Anna Rountree experienced, and her husband would journal and record her prophetic experiences. Incredible. One of the things I absolutely love about that particular book is that about a fourth of the book is endnotes—biblical references as confirmation of the experiences.

Or, how about some of the early books, in particular, by Rick Joyner? I read *The Harvest* when it was first published and it rocked my world—and it rocked the charismatic world too because it was a vision of things to come. And how about Joyner's *The Final Quest,* which is a revelatory journaling of his encounters with the Holy Spirit. *The Vision, The Harvest,* and *The Final Quest* were books leading up to *The Call.* Each are forms of modern-day revelatory journaling that were published to edify the Church.

Historical journaling is another dimension, but it isn't emphasized in the Spirit-filled, evangelical, Pentecostal, charismatic arenas—it's more popular in traditional churches. Historical journaling is documenting your lessons learned from life's journey. These journals are often referred to as diaries and one of the most common forms of journaling throughout time. Diaries can be extremely personal and intimate in nature and used to record historical events, wars, disasters, and well as romance and family matters.

Anne Frank: The Diary of a Young Girl reveals what everyday life was like going into and during World War II. It's an excellent example of journaling the way it's supposed to be. This diary is written to someone named Kitty—but I think this diary could have been written to you and to me. Each time I remember reading this book that chronicles two years of hiding from the Nazis in an attic with her family, the Holy Spirit floods me with His presence. Sharing her experiences in her diary no doubt brought her some relief from reality.

I encourage you to journal about your life—or perhaps the life of a grandparent who touched you with God's love or a miracle. This is historical journaling. Someone(s) needs to hear what you have to share. Whether praising God for all His blessings, or writing about your journey through the valley of the shadow of death, your own dark night, your encounters with God can later become a great encouragement to others not to sit in the valley, but to go *through* the valley.

Another excellent example of historical journaling is *Life and Diary of David Brainerd* by Jonathan Edwards. David Brainerd was one of the great apostolic statesmen missionaries in the United States to the First Nations people during the formation of the United States. All of his journaling, his daily diary entries, are included in this book. It's just incredible. I received so much encouragement. For example, an excerpt of his writing says:

> The Lord's Day, December 19th. At the sacrament of the Lord's Supper, seemed strong in the Lord; and the world, with all its frowns and flatteries, in a great measure disappeared so that my soul had nothing to do with them. I felt a disposition to be holy and forever the Lord's.

Do you want to be holy and forever the Lord's? This is historic journaling. This is a diary—recording lessons from life.

Another historical figure who kept a diary is George Washington. During my research for a webinar, I discovered the book *George Washington's Diaries*. I didn't even know that he journaled and when I found this book, I was amazed. (By the way, all these books are listed in Recommended Reading for your reference.) I have all of the writings of Abraham Lincoln, too.

Sometimes journaling can encompass all three dimensions: devotional, revelatory, and historical. You may journal about a book you read about Charles Spurgeon, or after attending a conference where the speaker was especially interesting. How you see the world that day or see the Lord through events of a given day is worth writing about. Each day is a gift worth saving in your treasure chest.

Matthew 13:52 Jesus says: "*Therefore **every scribe** instructed concerning the kingdom of heaven is like a householder who brings out of his **treasure things new and old**"* (NKJV).

I have recorded treasures in my journals. I have my late wife's recorded treasures. And someday somebody is going to inherit these treasures.

Years ago I read *A Diary of Signs and Wonders* by Maria Woodworth-Etter. This has become a classic written by an unusual woman in church history who moved in incredible signs and wonders. When I first read it, I didn't know that those kinds of God encounters still happened—but because she was faithful to record some of the most amazing revelatory encounters in her diary, we can encounter God too through her journaling.

A PERSONAL TOUCH

I've carried a roller bag around with me for years. My Bible's in it, my laptop, sermon notes, all kinds of stuff. And, a journal is always in it too. I may not write in it every day, but it is definitely part of my must-haves when I walk out the door.

Someone recently at the church I attend said, "I've noticed that you always take notes during the sermon." He said it as though other people don't—and most don't in today's church. In fact, a lot of people don't even take a Bible along to church because Scripture is flashed onto a huge screen, so people don't even have to open their Bibles. This can make lazy Christians. Does that sound harsh? Maybe it is, but it's the truth.

Some Christians today don't even know what books are in the Old or the New Testaments, let alone where they are located. Don't be a spoon-fed believer. In fact, one of the great things to do is journal what you are reading from the Word of God—the Bible—and how it is speaking to you. Sounds good, doesn't it!

Journaling has been part of my life for many years. I wasn't always the most consistent, but when I heard from God, learned a valuable lesson or received a revelation, I wrote it down. I've written journals on the Journal of an Adventurous Man. After my wife passed away, I wrote a journal on a laptop and tried to call it The Journal of a Hopeful Man, but I wasn't really there yet.

Even to the grocery store, everywhere I go, I have a journal with me—and believe me, one of these days, a glorious treasure chest of life overflowing from the heart will be complete and left behind.

WRITE DOWN POINTS THAT MATTER

*I will stand on my guard post and station myself on the rampart; and **I will keep watch to see what He will speak to me**, and how I may reply when I am reproved. Then the Lord answered me and said, "**Record the vision and inscribe it on tablets**, that the one who reads it may run"* (Habakkuk 2:1-2).

From these two verses there are seven points that matter:

1. Take your place.

2. Be watchful.

3. Believe God wants to speak to you.

4. A pure heart motivation is everything.

5. Write it down!

6. Be ready to move into an appropriate application.

7. Preserve His word for the days to come.

First we are told to stand guard—to station ourselves on the "rampart," a protective barrier. We are to be as soldiers dedicated to holding our ground in anticipation of hearing from our almighty Commander in Chief. We are told to stand still and listen for God to speak—He may have something to tell us, to correct in us. Maybe our character or lack of faith needs to be put right. When He tells us through a vision, we are to record it by writing it down.

One day I heard the Lord speak to me while I was journaling about taking a vacation. It was a word to me in a specific time that I needed for my soul to rest. I wrote it down and I obeyed—what a wonderful time of refreshment that was! He spoke to me as I journaled. Fascinating.

We are to be watchful too. It's so very easy to be distracted these days—so many activities that want our attention. But when we're watchful for the Lord to speak, we focus on what really matters. Believing that He really wants to communicate with us is crucial. Doubt may try and creep up the rampart, but stand firm on faith in Him. With a pure heart you will be motivated to keep a righteous life—and the Voice will be heard.

And remember, if the vision tarries, it's because the appointed, specific time has yet to arrive. And if it arrives but seems not to be for you personally, it could be for those who read the vision later—and because you were faithful to record it, they become the ones who run with your call. That's what these verses mean to me.

A Personal Touch

The heading of this section is from the hymn, "Blessed Assurance." Often hymns are a form of journaling. Songwriting, poetry, screenplays—there can be many creative dimensions that will open to you if you sit with Him for a while and write. Some of my assignments from the Lord on what I teach at conferences and in my webinars have come in a dream—which I wrote down immediately. This is revelatory journaling.

Although I have authored several dozen books, I don't have a background in writing. During my life journey, though, I had kept notes, a form of journaling. One time in a dream, the Holy Spirit showed me the front cover of a book. Then I saw the Table of Contents. It was so exciting! In this dream I saw the cover and could read the contents page. (This only happened once, but, Lord, do it again!) Next I remember reading the first page of the second chapter. When I woke up, I remembered all that I saw in the dream and I quickly wrote it down. If I hadn't, it would have been a fleeting memory.

Then what happened? The first page of the second chapter became the basis of my book *Kneeling on the Promises,* which became my *The Prophetic Intercessor* book, that is today *Praying with God's Heart*—all written as a result of revelatory journaling. Yes, I did.

This is my story. I journaled sermon notes of others, as well as dreams and visions in the night. My wife recorded portions of her nine straight weeks of angelic visitations. As mentioned previously, I have journaled on my laptop. I've written in inexpensive spiral notebooks as well as penned in beautiful leather-bound journals. I also have photo albums with commentary added and home-recorded videos that serve as journals. I take notes on my phone, too. Each of these journals holds a distinct, appropriate, and special place in my life journey.

In fact, one morning I had a raw dream about journaling that took me through some of my life's experiences. I was shown some of the trauma and hurt and pain and rejection I had gone through. I was actually weeping in my dream. It wondered, "Why are You doing this, Holy Spirit?" It was fascinating because the dream was interactive—the revelatory dimension, a divine exchange.

I woke up with a new assignment from God. One that I am just getting started on. It came to me the next morning. He told me, "I want you to journal as a tool of healing, to journal your recovery from trauma." That's devotional. That's revelatory. And it may be historical—a very intimate diary.

Journaling can lead to writing a memoir or your autobiography. Frances "Fanny" Crosby was a writer of more than 8,000 hymns, including "Blessed Assurance." She also wrote poems, a memoir, *Memories of Eighty Years,* and eventually penned her autobiography. Although she was blind from shortly after birth, she was an American mission worker, composer, lyricist, teacher—and journal writer.

Christian classics include *The Journal of John Wesley,* which spans fifty years of his life and includes his thoughts, feelings, and devotion to the Gospel of Jesus Christ and *The Prayers of Susanna Wesley,* which is a compilation of beautiful prayers of the mother of John and Charles Wesley, important Christian men in the 1700s who no doubt benefited from her prayers and that they were recorded to bless others as well.

Charles Finney, the leader in the Second Great Awakening in the United States and called the Father of Modern Revivalism, also wrote of his life journey. Others who kept journals include Marie Curie, Mark Twain, Winston Churchill, Albert Einstein. And some well-knowns who wrote autobiographies include Billy Graham, Ronald Reagan, Michelle Obama,

Nelson Mandela, Mahatma Gandhi, Andre Agassi, Dick Van Dyke, and Lucille Ball.

WHICH FORM IS BEST?

You may ask, "Which dimension of journaling is the best?" Well, that's like asking which of the gifts of the Spirit are best—healings, knowledge, revelation, prophecy, miracles? The answer: the one that is needed at the moment.

So, in your walk with God, you need to be flexible in His hands. Journaling should not be a rigid set of rules, but rather a tool in the Master's hand. As the dream that I have journaled states, "Do what matters. Just do it."

EMPOWERING PRAYER

As you begin this book, I hope and pray you will do so with an open mind and heart. I'm committed to sharing with you how journaling can change your relationship with your heavenly Father for the better. Please take ownership of the following prayer and pray it from your heart and spirit:

> Father, in the great name of Jesus, I present myself to You. May the Holy Spirit touch me right now with His peace and comfort and wisdom. Sometimes I feel stuck in my spiritual life, almost like my heart has been clogged or even some of it has been shut down. And Father, I want to grow in greater communion with You. I want to be a wise steward of Your revelatory ways, and I want to learn lessons from my life's journey. Therefore, I submit myself to You—Your will and Your word and Your ways. I am asking that You lead me into the right application of journaling that fits into the current season of my life. I want to record the dreams You have for me—

big dreams. I need to dream with You, God. So, please lead me into the right application of journaling that fits into the current season of my life. I'm excited and looking forward to encountering You, God, through my journaling. Give me the pen of the ready writer as my heart overflows with a good theme, and I address my verses to You, the King above all kings.

ENDNOTE

1. Madame Jeanne-Marie Bouvier was a French Roman Catholic mystic and writer, a central figure in the theological debates of 17th-century French, advocating an extreme passivity, wherein she believed that one became an agent of God. https://www.britannica.com/biography/Jeanne-Marie-Bouvier-de-La-Motte-Guyon-Madame-du-Chesnoy; accessed March 7, 2020.

SECTION TWO

KEYS TO THE JOURNEY

INTRODUCTION

Then the Lord answered me and said, "Write the vision and make it plain on tablets, that he may run who reads it"

(HABAKKUK 2:2 NKJV).

VISION

D o you need help retaining the revelation you receive from God? I have a simple remedy for you—journal! Yes, it is one of those awesome spiritual disciplines—a tried and tested spiritual tool that helps you retain revelation and grow in your capacity to discern the voice of the Holy Spirit.

Journaling is a fundamental and clearly useful biblical tool to help you preserve and be more faithful with what He speaks to you.

Throughout this book you will learn how a clear vision of the purpose of journaling will enhance your spiritual life, which will impact your physical, mental, relational, work, and family life.

There are several keys to journaling that you will learn in this section of the book—beginning with three distinct expressions of journaling:

1.   Dialoguing devotionally with God

2. Recording revelatory experiences

3. Documenting lessons from your life journey

In additional to the keys, there are three questions to ask yourself as you move forward in discovering how best to journal your life's journey:

1. Are you expectant? Do you expect revelation as you think about experiences and write about them?

2. Are you prepared? Have you considered the time and effort as well as the rewards you will receive if you take on this very special and new aspect of life?

3. Are you a student? Will you look at each moment, day, month, year and beyond as lessons in life from which you will learn how to best maneuver for His glory and your benefit?

In this section we will also discuss the three nuances of the nature of revelation:

1. Revelation is partial

2. Revelation is progressive

3. Revelation is conditional

Of course there is always the question: Why should I devote my time to journaling? Well, for one thing, it will please God, as you are committing time and devotion to communing and communicating with Him, your heavenly Father. And for another reason, there are practical applications for your life that will bring you blessings. When God speaks, it is always best to listen.

I will stand on my guard post and station myself on the rampart; and I will keep watch to see what He will speak to me, and how I may reply when I am reproved (Habakkuk 2:1).

From Habakkuk you learn to:

+ Take your place and stand firm.

+ Be ever watchful for Him.

+ Believe He wants to speak to you.

+ Listen to your heart—heart motivation is everything.

+ Be ready to move into an appropriate application of what He tells you.

Other practical matters include:

+ Keep a notepad and pen by your bed.

+ Grammar and neatness are not critical issues.

+ Consider using a small digital recording device.

+ Word-process your key revelations later so you can have them as you travel.

+ Learn to discern your revelatory alphabet by keeping track of symbols.

+ Make a note of your feelings and emotions when an experience occurs.

+ Be still and try to recall one or two of the details.

+ Date all entries.

+ Record your location—it all matters.

- Expect God's love to be affirmed toward you!

A Personal Touch

In my journey with the Holy Spirit, I have done all three major forms of journaling. Which one is right is like asking, "Which gift of the Spirit is the most important?" A good answer can be, "The one that is needed at the moment!" In your life and walk with God, be flexible in His hands. Don't let journaling become a rigid law or rule—but rather a tool in the Master's hand. Do what matters. Just do it!

Combining the three expressions of journaling, asking and answering those three essential questions, and considering the three nuances of revelation gave me every spiritual tool necessary to receive and then reveal, through journaling, God's pure and pristine love for me. My spirit was open to clearly hear the Holy Spirit's guiding voice.

Points that Matter

Receiving Pure Revelation

There is a pure river of God. Revelation is clear and pure in its origin. The problems are the tainted filters on our end that need to be cleansed and made whole. God wants the revelation coming out of us to be as pure as the revelation coming out of us.

Significance of Quietness

Learning the lessons of quieting your soul before God is a major key. We are to walk in and maintain the center of quiet in the midst of a chaotic world. Have you learned to quiet your soul in order to commune with God?

Being Secure in God

A realistic tension exists between being sensitive to the Holy Spirit and not being reactive to the corrections of others. We must find our security and identity in our relationship with our loving Heavenly Father.

Journaling is Relational—Not a Professional Performance

This is personal. This is not about how neat or how grammatically correct your journaling is. This is not about your performance level. No matter the expression of your journaling, it is about cultivating an intimate relationship with your maker.

Journaling Is a Tool

Basically, journaling is simply a method of keeping notes for future reference. It can take many forms. Your journal may consist of your prayers, a record of God's answers as you perceive them, and/or a record of what you sense the Holy Spirit is saying to you through His various delivery systems.

Is it a Discipline or a Privilege?

When teaching on spiritual disciplines one time, the voice of the Holy Spirit interrupted me in the middle of my presentation. "Spiritual disciplines? Spiritual disciplines? You do not have enough discipline to have a spiritual discipline! They are spiritual privileges, anyway!" This revelation changed my orientation and inner motivation. I now saw these as tools of a birthright and an honor, not a legalistic work for approval. They are a privilege!

EMPOWERING PRAYER

Father, in the wonderful name of Jesus, I present myself to You. I want to grow in the Spirit of revelation. Therefore, I submit myself to You and I ask that You lead me into the right application of journaling that fits the current season of my life. I call forth the empowering work of the Holy Spirit to make my journaling effective. And Father, I declare that I want to grow in the Spirit of Wisdom and Revelation. Give me keys in receiving and retaining revelation. Thank You for the honor and the privilege of writing down the vision, realizing that this does not only affect my life but also those around me. I declare that I will receive revelation that will result in a lineage and legacy being established. Thank You for more lessons in Your School of the Holy Spirit. Amen and amen!

RECEIVING PURE REVELATION

How can we know if a word is genuine? It is too easy to dismiss a word as being "off" simply because we do not consider all of the factors.

First, we must evaluate the source of the word. Let's say that you are learning how to use your prophetic gift and a thought crosses your mind. Simply because you are a prophet, does that mean it is from God? Not necessarily. We must learn to discern the difference between three different voices that can sometimes sound almost the same: God's Holy Spirit, our own thoughts, and satan.

John advises us to *"test the spirits to see whether they are from God"* (1 John 4:1). How should we do that? We cannot test a word by its fruits yet, if it has not been delivered, but we can anticipate its results to some extent. Will the word express God's love to the hearers, even as it convicts them? Or will it bring them condemnation and hopelessness? Are your own emotions and opinions part of the mix? Have you left an opening for the devil in your own life lately?

Jeremiah wrote, *"I have not sent these prophets, yet they run around claiming to speak for me. I have given them no message, yet they go on prophesying"* (Jeremiah 23:21 NLT; see also Ezekiel 13:1-2). People can speak out of personal desire or ambition or a sense of urgency. We all know what it feels like to speak out of an unsanctified place in our hearts.

Just because something comes to us in a "spiritual" way does not guarantee that it comes from a pure source. Satan is a spirit, too, and he is deceptive by nature. *"This is the spirit of the antichrist,"* wrote John (1 John 4:3). Even one of Jesus' premier disciples, Peter, had to suffer a rebuke from the Lord "Get behind Me, Satan!"—really a rebuke of the evil spirit who had incited him to say, *"God forbid it, Lord! This shall never happen to You"* (Matthew 16:22-23).

If you're just not sure, the wisest course of action is to either hold on to the word until you know what to do with it, or to present it with qualifications ("It seems that God might be saying something like this....")

The written Word of God is always the best test of any word of revelation. As the psalm tells us: *"Your word is a lamp to my feet and a light to my path"* (Psalm 119:105). In particular, a word will more likely be genuine if a prophet has been studying the Word and letting it inform his or her thoughts and judgments. A good example is the prophet Daniel, who wrote:

> *It was the first year of the reign of Darius the Mede, the son of Ahasuerus, who became king of the Babylonians. During the first year of his reign, I, Daniel, learned from reading the word of the Lord, as revealed to Jeremiah the prophet, that Jerusalem must lie desolate for seventy years* (Daniel 9:1-2 NLT).

His attention was on the message of the Word of God, and he humbled himself to know more. He meditated on the written Word for a long time. He resisted the fearful uncertainty that the evil one sent his way. And he got it right; his prophetic words and actions brought about the fulfillment of the very Word of God.

As we have already explored, words from God do not come to us only as thoughts that are meant to be spoken. The Lord makes His words known to us in a wide range of ways, including visions, dreams, parables (see Hosea 12:10), "dark sayings" (see Psalm 78:2; Proverbs 1:6), natural things (see Jeremiah 18), angelic encounters, and, as He did with Moses, face to face (see Numbers 12:8).

The mode of revelation is not as important as the message. If God wants to get His word across, He will use the most appropriate means to do it. *"Hear now My words: if there is a prophet among you, I, the Lord, shall make Myself known to him in a vision. I shall speak with him in a dream"* (Numbers 12:6).

PRACTICAL APPLICATIONS
OF QUIETNESS

A re you ready for one of the most hidden and significant keys to unlocking the world of revelation in your life?

One primary principle in retaining revelation is to learn to be still before the Lord—to quiet our mind and spirit and wait on Him. It says in Psalm 46:10 (KJV), *"Be still, and know that I am God."* Years ago, the Holy Spirit taught me that stillness is the incubation bed of revelation. Quietness can actually be a form of faith because it is the opposite of anxiety and worry. Many times that is easier said than done. So, just how do you learn to become still before God?

I'll try to answer. First, remove external distractions. Mark 1:35 says that Jesus went to a secluded place to pray. Find a place where you can get away. For me, when I was growing up, I would get away by taking long walks. My family lived in a rural community in northwest Missouri. There were railroad tracks less than 300 yards from our house, and I used to get on those tracks and walk for miles. Hour after hour I would walk and talk to God. Outdoors and alone was the best place for me to have my communal time with the lover of my soul. Distractions were minimal. I could talk to God and listen to Him talk to me.

I have to fight for this alone time today. But whether it is a walk in the hills of Franklin, Tennessee, lingering in my bed with the covers pulled over my head, sitting in my special chair, or quieting my soul while listening to my favorite soaking CD, nothing takes the place of time alone with God!

Second, you must quiet your inner being. One of the biggest challenges in this will be your mind's tendency to suddenly remember all sorts of things that you need to do. The best way to counter that is by taking a few moments to write down all those things so that you can remember to do them later. Then, put them out of your head. Your mind should be at rest on those matters because you have taken action and not simply tried to ignore them. Release your personal tensions and anxieties to the Lord, *"casting all your anxiety on Him, because He cares for you"* (1 Peter 5:7). Finally, focus your meditating on the person of Jesus. Yes, focus on Jesus!

In becoming still, you are not trying to do anything. You simply want to be in touch with your Divine Lover, Jesus. Center on this moment of time and experience Him in it. All of these things will help you silence the inner noise of voices, thoughts, pressures, etc., that otherwise would force their way to the top. This grace of becoming still before God is often referred to as contemplative prayer.

Quietness has a great deal to do with your having a spirit of revelation in your life. Commit yourself to creating a spiritual culture where the Holy Dove will want to come and stay. Pull down the shades over the windows of your soul. Enter the Holy of Holies in your heart where Jesus the Messiah lives. Yes, He has taken up residence within you! He is there, and He is waiting to commune with you.

You are now a candidate to receive revelation! In some way, *Rhema* is couched in vision. The Book of Habakkuk opens with the words, *"The oracle* [or burden] *which Habakkuk the prophet saw"* (Habakkuk 1:1). The prophet quieted himself to watch and see what the Lord would speak. As we have seen, focusing the eyes of our heart upon God causes us to become inwardly still. It raises our level of faith and expectancy and results in our being more fully open to receive from God.

WISDOM WAYS WITH JOURNALING

Any venture into new territory is fraught with perils and pitfalls; receiving and retaining revelation is no different. Here are some practical safeguards to help protect you as you embark on your adventure.

1. Cultivate a humble, teachable spirit. Never allow the attitude, "God told me, and that's all there is to it." All revelation is to be tested. You will make mistakes. Accept that as a part of the learning process and go on.

2. Have a good working knowledge of the Bible. Remember, *Rhema* is based on *Logos*. The revelatory never conflicts with the written Word!

3. God primarily gives revelation for the area in which He has given responsibility and authority. *Look for revelation in areas of your responsibility.* Stay away from ego trips that motivate you to seek revelation for areas in which God has not yet placed you.

4. Walk together with others. Realize that until your guidance is confirmed, it should be regarded as what you think God is saying.

5. Realize that if you submit to God and resist the devil, he *must* flee from you! You can trust the guidance of the Holy Spirit to lead you into truth.

Add this tool of journaling to your "tool box" and you will mature in the grace of retaining revelation and the capacity of discerning God's voice. As you get ready to begin, you may wish to pray a prayer like this one:

> "Father, grant me the grace to journal, in Jesus' great name. Teach me the skills of how to retain revelation and clearly discern the flow of Your voice. Lead me in Your wisdom applications of recording what You reveal. In Jesus' wonderful name, amen."

Now, let's just do it! Experience is always the best teacher!

BEING SECURE IN GOD

A s a prophetic person, each of us needs to be like a rhinoceros— thick-skinned but with a big, sensitive heart. For too long I have been *thin*-skinned with a big heart. I have learned the hard way about feeling rejected because of my prophetic sensibilities and the primary lesson I have learned is that my flow of revelation will slow to a trickle if I do not get up when I have been knocked down. I have learned that I always need the main and plain truth of the Gospel more than I may think. The way of the Cross leads home, and through Jesus we each have a personal place of belonging.

The truth is that Jesus was punished for our sin that we might be forgiven (see Isaiah 53:9-12). He was wounded for our sicknesses that we might be healed. *"By his wounds we are healed"* (Isaiah 53:5 NIV). He became poor for our sakes that we might have His wealth. Our Lord died that we might have His life. (Read all of Isaiah 53—the ringing declaration of the divine exchange.) We have been accepted, adopted, and cared for. God does not only tolerate us, He fully embraces and loves us (see Ephesians 1:5-6; 3:14-15; John 1:12–13). After all, He created us. He *always* has time for each and every one of us.

Accept the fact that you are fully accepted in Christ. Lay down your bitterness and forgive those who have rejected you. Instead of returning evil for evil or withdrawing to lick your wounds, sow a blessing. Search out Scriptures that reinforce the fact that you are accepted in Christ, loved with an everlasting love that does not depend upon your performance. Let the Spirit of God transform your mind. (To begin with, read Romans 12.) Part of belonging to Him is to suffer rejection along with Him, and that suffering knits us even more closely with Him:

> So you have not received a spirit that makes you fearful slaves. Instead, you received God's Spirit when he adopted you as his own children. Now we call him, "Abba, Father." For his Spirit joins with our spirit to affirm that we are God's children. And since we are his children, we are his heirs. In fact, together with Christ we are heirs of God's glory. **But if we are to share his glory, we must also share his suffering** (Romans 8:15-17 NLT).

Accept yourself. Recognize that *"we are His workmanship, created in Christ Jesus for good works, which God prepared beforehand so that we would walk in them"* (Ephesians 2:10). Did you know that it is not humility to criticize yourself? It is rebellion. We find it in the Bible: *"Who are you, a human being, to talk back to God? Shall what is formed say to the one who formed it, 'Why did you make me like this?'"* (Romans 9:20 NIV). So take yourself in hand. Repent and break off any word curses you may have pronounced on yourself. If your difficulties seem to be intractable, consider the possibility of seeking prayer for deliverance; at the least seek counsel from others concerning this issue.[1]

I believe that if we are following in His footsteps, we should expect to be dishonored instead of expecting to be honored. That should make every rejection an honor and a privilege instead of a cause for offense and outrage.

We belong to our Master, Jesus, and He suffered utter rejection. We know because He said, *"My God, My God, why have You forsaken Me?"* (Matthew 27:46 NKJV). By comparison, anything we suffer is insignificant. I do not know your journey with every step of its perils and power. I do know the pits and pinnacles of the prophetic lifestyle and I believe I have been part of helping to change the equilibrium in the Body of Christ.

Fifty or sixty years ago, nobody talked about the place of prophecy in an everyday congregation; now it comes up all the time. This groundswell may still seem small compared to the number of congregations in the worldwide Body of Christ, but it appears to be growing steadily. As we lift up the Lord Jesus Christ, and honor the prophetic word, let's do our part to contribute to the health of His Church.

EMPOWERING PRAYER

Father, in the healing name of Jesus, we direct our gaze to You. We find our purpose and meaning in life, not from our gifts and callings, but from being Your sons and daughters. Help us to grow into maturity in our prophetic callings while learning how to walk and work together with others, effectively and in love. We look to You as our source of validation and we offer ourselves to be servant leaders in the Body of Christ and to any sphere of influence into which you lead us. Thank You for teaching us through the pioneers who have gone before us. In You, we live! Amen.

NOTE

1. You can consult my book *Deliverance from Darkness* for more on this subject.

WORDS ARE RELATIONAL NOT PROFESSIONAL

The most powerful prophetic words are relational, not professional. Reaching out with acts of kindness may be the best prophetic ministry of all, and you certainly do not have to punctuate every word with "thus saith the Lord." Feel free to change your language, making it less religious and more ordinary, more approachable. I will have much more to say about this as the following chapters unfold.

Let love be your aim (see 1 Corinthians 14:1). Love is the conduit that carries faith. You do not have to be a know-it-all. Just be a genuine person who cares about people. Ask questions and get to know people. Learn to move in the gifts of the Spirit as you grow in the fruit of the Spirit (love, joy, peace, patience, kindness, gentleness, and self-control—see Galatians 5:22-23).

It is a process. Like an eaglet, you were not hatched knowing how to soar or hunt. Even when you reach maturity, you will have to learn new things. Just remember that you have the best Teacher you could possibly have, and that He has promised to perfect the work He has begun in you (see Philippians 1:6). He will also recondition you all along the way, much like the way He reconditions the feathers of a molting eagle.

Never forget your goal, which is the goal for anyone who is called by His name: to exalt Jesus. After John was invited into the heavenly throne room, he recorded these words: *"The testimony of Jesus is the spirit of prophecy"* (Revelation 19:10). What is important is not the sweep of your wingspan or the accuracy of your eye. What matters is that you train your eagle eyes to keep your focus on Jesus Himself. As an eagle of God, are you releasing His testimony?

EMPOWERING PRAYER

Father, in Jesus' great name, we want to see a prophetic company rise up with their hearts set on You. Help us to pursue love and yet earnestly desire the gift of prophecy. Give us prophetic hearts so that we can release the testimony of Jesus to all those with whom we come into contact. May we have the eyes of eagles to discern our prey and learn to swoop down for the capture. Increase our wingspan so that we can soar to new heights. We declare that we are no longer an endangered species and that we do not have to live in fear. Yes, like the eagles, we now dare to fly higher than ever before! Amen.

JOURNALING AS A TOOL OF RETAINING REVELATION

D o you need help retaining what you have already received? Then I have a simple remedy for you—journal! Yes, it is one of those awesome spiritual disciplines! Journaling is a tried and tested spiritual tool that will help you retain revelation and grow in your capacity to discern the voice of the Holy Spirit. I have tried it, and it works!

Basically, journaling is simply a method of keeping notes for future reference. It can take many forms. Your journal may consist of your prayers, a record of God's answers as you perceive them, and/or a record of what you sense the Holy Spirit is saying to you through His various delivery systems. Journaling is a fundamental and clearly useful biblical discipline.

Some believers express concern that journaling is an attempt to put subjective revelation on the same level of authority as Scripture. This is not the case at all. The Bible alone is the infallible Word of God. Journaling is just another tool to help us retain and be more faithful with what He speaks to us.

God speaks to His children much of the time! However, we do not always differentiate His voice from our own thoughts, and thus we are timid at times about stepping out in faith. If we clearly learn to retain what He is speaking to us, we will know that He has already confirmed His voice and Word to us. Thus we will be enabled to walk out God's words to us with greater confidence. Journaling then becomes a way of sorting out God's thoughts from our own.

As it has been for so many, the simple art of recording revelation may prove to be one of the missing links in your own walk of hearing God's voice. Continuity of language, divine suggestions and reminders, and also learning the proper interpretation of symbols will occur as you use journaling as a creative tool of storing up and later deciphering revelation.

I strongly encourage you to start journaling now if you have not already done so. The principles, tips, and suggestions in this chapter will help you get off to a strong start. Those of you who are already engaged in journaling, I urge you to continue!

To encourage you as to the value of journaling, let me share some thoughts on the subject from another elder friend, Herman Riffel. Herman is one of the "patriarchs" of modern-day visionary revelation—an authority not only on dreams and their interpretation but also on journaling as an effective method of retaining revelation.

> In life we keep the treasures we value. Unwanted mail that comes is tossed away with just a glance. But bills, whether we like them or not, are carefully laid aside until we pay them. Checks are deposited in the bank so that no money is lost. Diplomas and certificates of recognition are hung on the wall for others to see.
>
> What do we do with the promises the Lord gives us? They are worth more than any amount of money. What happens to the lessons we have learned through difficult and costly experiences? Too often we forget within a day or two

the words of encouragement God gave us. The promises vanish away in the midst of new problems, unless we make a proper record of them.

I know by personal experience. Lillie and I pray for our children regularly, often for specific needs. Then we wait on the Lord for His answer, and graciously He gives us a word of encouragement.

Recently one of these words came to us: *Salvation shall spring forth like the grass and you will rejoice with joy unspeakable, for I will do what I have promised. Therefore, wait in patience and trust in Me, for I am faithful.*

This was an encouraging word and we did rejoice in it. Just a few days later, however, I asked Lillie if she remembered what the promise was that God had given. She did not remember, and neither did I, for problems had absorbed our attention again. Since I keep a journal, however, we were able to check it, find the promise, and again receive encouragement.[1]

A Personal Note

One of the treasures I found upon the departure of my dear late wife, Michal Ann, was her personal, revelatory journals, sitting in her nightstand beside our bed. To my delight, I found the original handwritten notes telling of her nine weeks of angelic visitations in the early 1990s. In it she wrote how the Holy Spirit promised her that next time He came to visit her, not only would the angels come, but Jesus Himself would come for her. It brought such comfort to me to realize this is exactly what had happened. Jesus Himself had come for her. Her journals gave me comfort, insight, and hope.

Therefore, I urge you to begin keeping a journal if you are not already doing so. What to include in a personal spiritual revelatory journal? One of the first things we may record in the day are our dreams from the night before. Some use digital recorders and others use computers; devices today help in the journaling experience. I still use notebooks and " journals" for the most part. I write down the date, the place I am in, the time I woke up and the summary of the experience.

Often later, I reflect on it, after prayer and waiting on the Lord, and compose a short potential application of the prophetic experience.

We may record a Scripture which God speaks to us that day. A burden, a heartfelt urgency as well as dreams and visions and visitations may be noted. You see, your journal is a track record of your spiritual adventure, not simply a diary to record daily activities. So we take time to listen to what God is saying to our hearts. We might meditate on the Scriptures, or we might sit in contemplation before our Lord Jesus Himself. We learn to "waste time on Jesus," from the world's viewpoint, in order to hear what God wants to say to us.

I'm glad my Annie left me a journal! Now I have a treasure chest full of jewels that I can go back to and glean the many lessons He was teaching us those many years ago. The Lost Art of Journaling is a key to receiving and retaining revelation. Ready to start? Let's get going!

NOTE

1. Herman H. Riffel, *Learning to Hear God's Voice* (Old Tappan, NJ: Chosen Books, 1986), 147-148.

DISCIPLINE OR PRIVILEGE?

S uch is the principle of journaling. Obviously, there are many different forms of journaling. Our focus in this book is on journaling our
dream and vision language, but we can journal many other aspects of
our Christian lives. There are prayer journals and daily devotional journals,
for example. People keep different types of journals for different purposes.

Some people would describe journaling as a spiritual discipline. I prefer another term. Like many others, I have used the phrase "spiritual discipline" for years to describe any habitual practice we undertake to facilitate
spiritual growth. When composing my book *The Lost Art of Practicing
His Presence,* however, the Holy Spirit said to me, "You're not disciplined
enough to have a spiritual discipline." That nailed me!

"Okay," I replied, surprised and a little miffed. (Deep in my heart,
though, I knew He was right.)

He said, "These are spiritual privileges." That put a whole new angle
on things. I really like the phrase, "spiritual privileges," because that is what
they are. Looking at them as privileges rather than as disciplines completely
changes your mindset because doing something as a discipline can sometimes lead to a performance-based mentality. Doing the same thing as a

privilege, however, means doing it because you can do it, because you see the value in doing it, because God enables you to do it, and because you want to do it—not because you have to do it to please God or stay on His "good side." It becomes a matter of perspective, like the difference between saying the glass is half empty or half full. Praying, studying, fasting, worshiping—they are all amazing spiritual privileges—with great benefits!

LESSONS FROM HABAKKUK AND DANIEL

Journaling our spiritual experiences has clear biblical precedent. Several times in the Book of Revelation, John is instructed to record what he sees. In fact, the entire Book of Revelation itself is a divinely inspired record of a series of awesome and incredible visions that John saw while *in the Spirit on the Lord's day*" (Revelation 1:10).

The discipline of spiritual journaling appears also in the Old Testament. Consider, for example, these words from the prophet Habakkuk:

> *I will stand on my guard post and station myself on the rampart; and I will keep watch to see what He will speak to me, and how I may reply when I am reproved. Then the Lord answered me and said, "Record the vision and inscribe it on tablets, that the one who reads it may run. For the vision is yet for the appointed time; it hastens toward the goal and it will not fail. Though it tarries, wait for it; for it will certainly come, it will not delay"* (Habakkuk 2:1-3).

Habakkuk is seeking a spiritual experience. He is seeking to hear the *rhema* voice of God directly in his heart so that he can understand what he sees around him. First of all, he goes to a quiet place where he can be alone and become still. Second, he quiets himself within by watching to see what God would say. Last of all, when God begins to speak, the first thing He says is, *"Record the vision."* Habakkuk wrote down what he was sensing in his heart. The benefits of this type of journaling were retained for years to come so that those who would later read it would be able to run with it. Often the vision is fulfilled by others, so here we have another great benefit: If the revelation is preserved, then another group, city, or even generation can learn the lessons and move forward themselves.

Daniel was another biblical prophet who journaled. In fact, the seventh chapter of the Book of Daniel is essentially Daniel's journal entry regarding a significant and powerful dream:

> *In the first year of Belshazzar king of Babylon Daniel saw a dream and visions in his mind as he lay on his bed; then he wrote the dream down and related the following summary of it* (Daniel 7:1).

If you read Daniel's account of his dream in the rest of the chapter, you'll find that Daniel did not write down all the details of his amazing and rather intense dream. While in a spirit of rest, he composed a summary of his encounter. Too many people get caught up in the microscopic details in their sincere attempts at journaling and thus end up missing the primary emphasis of their visitation. Be like Daniel—write down a summary and keep it simple! The Holy Spirit will have a way of bringing back to your remembrance the details you might need later.

I take enormous encouragement from the life of Daniel. His style of journaling particularly appeals to me. Daniel's life spanned almost the entire 70-year period of the Babylonian exile. The events recorded in the Book of Daniel cover much of that same period of time, yet it is only 12 chapters long. Obviously, Daniel did not record everything he experienced; or, at least, not everything he recorded has survived to come down to us today. The Book of Daniel records the highlights, the most spiritually significant events in the life of Daniel and his people. A lifetime of experience is condensed into 12 short chapters—a summary, as it were.

When it comes to journaling, here's the bottom line: Do what works for you. I can give you plenty of practical tips, but in the end you have to decide what you feel most comfortable with. Perhaps you like to write and are good at it; you may prefer to record a full account of your dreams and experiences. However, if you lack the time or inclination to write long accounts, do what Daniel and other prophets did and write a summary. Set down the simplest, most basic sequence of events as a framework for recording in detail the highlights in the most salient or significant points. Whatever—make it simple, practical, and attainable. Amen and amen!

Tips on Remembering Revelation

Some people tell me that they do not hear from God in their lives—period! Others say they simply can't remember their revelatory experiences. Still others seem to remember only a fragment or portions of scattered images, which at the time do not seem to make much sense to them. But you were born to be a dreamer.

Sleep specialists tell us that everyone dreams for a period of time while in rapid eye movement (REM) sleep. So, in reality, all of us dream at some point every night. The issue then becomes one of knowing some practical tips and learning to rest under the anointing of the Holy Spirit in order to recall what we have been shown.

The Scriptures speak of the fleeting nature of dreams:

> *He flies away like a dream, and they cannot find him; even like a vision of the night he is chased away* (Job 20:8).

Daniel 2:1-47 expresses the frustration that Nebuchadnezzar, the king of Babylon, experienced as he received a detailed dream but could not recall it! The dream disturbed the king so much that he searched for relief and health! God heard his plea and sent Daniel who, after a season of seeking the face of God, related to the king not only his dream itself but also its interpretation. In reality, of course, it was God who revealed these things to Daniel. Daniel sought God's face, and God gave him the spirit of understanding. If you seek God's face the way Daniel did, God will do the same for you.

Of course, no commitment to journaling will do any good if you cannot remember your dreams. At this point, I would like to add a few practical tips for retaining revelation. These steps will enhance your ability to journal effectively and enable you to remember your dreams longer.

1. If possible, get rid of your loud alarm clock. Ask the Holy Spirit to help you wake up. Try to establish the habit of getting up at a set time. This requires discipline and will naturally be harder for some than for others.

2. Many dreams come between four and five o'clock in the morning. Whenever you awaken, learn to linger for a few minutes in a place of rest, if possible.

3. Instead of an alarm, consider waking to a clock radio tuned to soothing music. This is what I did for years. I got rid of the blaring alarm and woke up to classical music, which doesn't chase away dreams. Classical music actually helps create a soothing atmosphere conducive to dream retention. Worship music has the same effect, particularly the softer, more soaking, reflective styles.

Be prepared to record your revelations by observing a few practical tips:

1. Keep a notepad and a pen by the bed so you won't have to get up before you record your dream. A simple spiral notebook works fine.

2. This is a personal journal. Grammar, neatness, and spelling are not critical issues. Content is crucial!

3. Consider using a small tape recorder. Keep it by your bedside so that all you have to do is turn over and whisper into it.

4. Later in the day or week, consider word-processing the scribbles you previously captured. Some people transfer their experiences to a more permanent "journal." I keep both a personal dream journal and a ministry dream journal in my bag at all times!

5. Develop your dream alphabet by keeping track of symbols. Ask, "What does this symbol mean to me?" and "Can I find it in Scripture?"

6. Make note of your feelings/emotions in the dream/revelation. When you summarize your dream, be sure to describe how you felt during the dream, even if you include only a few words.

7. Be still and try to recall one or two of the details, and then your memory will kick in (see Zechariah 4:1-2). Find one thread of the dream and then, in prayer, gently pull and more will appear on your screen.

8. Date all entries. This is important for many reasons, not the least of which is keeping track of patterns or progressions that may occur in your dream journey.

9. If traveling, record your location at the time of your dream. This can be just as important as the date. The locale may prove to be highly significant to interpreting your dream.

10. Expect God's love to be affirmed toward you. And then, as you receive it, expect the gifts of the Holy Spirit to be in operation.

Whenever possible, seek training and wise counsel from gifted interpreters of dreams. Not everyone will have this capacity as well developed as others. Even in Scripture, Daniel and Joseph are the only ones who are specifically mentioned as having this gift. Just as in the New Testament we have the gift of speaking in tongues, but corresponding to it we have the gift of interpretation of tongues. Ask for the interpretation! You have not because you ask not! Just ask!

SECTION THREE

HANDLING REVELATORY REALMS

Interpreting Revelation

INTRODUCTION

*Then they said to him, "We have had a dream and there is no one to **interpret** it." Then Joseph said to them, "Do not interpretations belong to God? Tell it to me, please"*

(GENESIS 40:8).

*Beloved, do not believe every spirit, but **test** the spirits to see whether they are from God, because many false prophets have gone out into the world*

(1 JOHN 4:1).

VISION

What language do you speak? Have you learned your spiritual alphabet? Your spiritual alphabet will be unique to you. God will speak revelation to you according to the language you speak. Doctors, nurses, and other medical and health professionals have a language all their own, a technical vocabulary that untrained laypeople cannot understand. Music has a written language that is incomprehensible to anyone who has never been taught to read the symbols.

Whatever your language is, the Holy Spirit will speak to you in that language. Of course, I'm not talking so much about languages like English, French, German, Russian, or Spanish as I'm the "language" with which we interpret life. We each have a personal walk and, in a sense, a personal talk. Our spiritual alphabet, though similar, is unique to each person.

Regardless of how our individual alphabets differ, our basic approach to interpretation should be the same. Proper interpretation can occur on many levels. The following are three practical applications and simple steps for interpreting the revelation you receive from God:

1. Study the interpretation of words and symbols by researching their meaning as recorded in Scripture. Find out how biblical characters and other figures from the past interpreted these words and symbols. This is an excellent way to begin.

2. Effective interpretation is a skill that is learned over time and with experience. Your spiritual alphabet is unique to you. Journaling will help you capture your distinct pictures, grant understanding over time, and give wisdom for your journey.

3. Welcome the anointing, gifting and presence of the Holy Spirit. He will guide you into truth, keeping things safe yet adventurous, and pure yet unreligious.

Section Three also discusses how God's Word tells us we must prove all things and hold fast to what is good (see 1 Thessalonians 5:21). At all times we must seek the Lord's wisdom while refusing to use "wisdom" as an excuse for fear. We must be careful not to become offended at the genuine things that the Holy Spirit is doing, no matter how strange they may appear to us. Divine revelation and visionary experiences come in many different forms, and it is vital we understand how to discern the true from the false.

Discernment is desperately needed in the Body of Christ. We need a clear, clean stream of communion with God resulting in a clear, clean flow of God's Word coming through us. Satan's number-one weapon is deception, and the Church's number-one need is discernment. An extremely practical antidote and application is to be more impressed with the Word of God going into us than we are the word coming out of us, so store up the Word of God in your heart and soul so that you have a plumb line with which to judge or test subjective revelation.

A PERSONAL TOUCH

Some years ago I was traveling through the night by train from the Frankfurt, Germany, region to Rosenheim in southern Bavaria. I was in one of the sleeping cars but, unable to sleep, I spent much of my time praying in the Spirit. The Holy Spirit kept speaking to me over and over, "Where are My Daniels? Where are My Esthers? Where are My Josephs, and where are My Deborahs?"

After many years of pondering on this word, I believe that the Holy Spirit is on a quest to find believers He can work with—believers who will dream God's dreams at any cost, have a discerning spirit to properly interpret the times, and who learn to intercede out of a posture of revelation.

Along my life's journey I have learned not to add to the Holy Spirit's words. We have to learn to put our prejudices aside in order to receive and release *pure revelation*. Though there is an increase in gifted people today, there is also a rise of "diluted stuff" that comes from insecure people attempting to make their revelation bigger or more profound than it actually is. We need to learn when God has stopped talking and man has continued on. Some of us over the years have called this "hamburger helper"! God does not need our additives!

Points that Matter

In Section Three you will learn how to: keep interpretation simple; the basics for interpreting dreams; and how revelation is full of symbolism. A brief deeper look at each follows:

Keep Interpretation Simple

The following are eight simple points to help you go in the right direction:

1. God will often use familiar terms that you know (Matthew 4:19).

2. Ask the Holy Spirit for insight (Daniel 7:8; 8:15-16; Luke 2:19).

3. What is the central theme? What is the main thought?

4. What was the primary emotion?

5. Consecutive dreams often have similar meanings (Genesis 41:1-7, 25-31).

6. What are the primary colors?

7. Some revelation will only be understood in the future.

8. The key to proper interpretation is to ask questions!

Basics for Dream Interpreting

Analyze your dream by asking a series of basic questions:

- First, where are you in the dream? If you are in the observation mode, then the dream probably is not primarily about you. If you are an observer, then you will be a witness.

- Second, are you participating? This could indicate that this revelatory realm includes you but as a participant but not the central figure.

- Third, are you the central focus? Is everyone watching you? If you are the central focus of the dream, then this revelatory encounter is directly about you.

Revelation is Full of Symbolism

There are three realms of interpreting symbols:

1. Always go to the Scriptures first.

2. After Scripture, a second place to look for interpretation of your revelatory symbols is in colloquial expressions.

3. The third realm for interpreting these prophetic symbols comes from our own personal revelatory alphabet.

Testing the Spirits

It's important to take seriously the Word of God as recorded in First John 4:1-3:

> *Dear friends, do not believe every spirit, but **test the spirits to see whether they are from God**, because many false prophets have gone out into the world. This is how you can recognize the Spirit of God: Every spirit that acknowledges that Jesus Christ has come in the flesh is from God, but every spirit that does not acknowledge Jesus is not from God. This is the spirit of the antichrist, which you have heard is coming and even now is already in the world.*

Nine Scriptural Tests for Revelation

The following is a list of nine scriptural tests to test every revelation we receive for accuracy, authority, and validity:

1. Does the revelation edify, exhort, or console? (See 1 Corinthians 14:3)

2. Is it in agreement with God's Word? (See 2 Timothy 3:16)

3. Does it exalt Jesus Christ? (See John 16:4)

4. Does it have good fruit? (See Matthew 7:15-16)

5. If it predicts a future event, does it come to pass? (See Deuteronomy 18:20-22)

6. Does the prophetic prediction turn people toward God or away from Him? (See Deuteronomy 13:1-5)

7. Does it produce liberty or bondage? (See Romans 8:15)

8. Does it produce life or death? (See 2 Corinthians 3:6)

9. Does the Holy Spirit bear witness that it is true? (See 1 John 2:27)

EMPOWERING PRAYER

In the name of the Lord Jesus Christ, I declare that the God of revelation is also the God of interpretation of the revelation. Give me a fresh hunger for the Word of God so I can study to show myself approved by God. Teach me, Holy Spirit, practical applications to the art of interpretation. Help me to build and recognize my own personal spiritual alphabet. I declare I am maturing as a good steward of these holy ways of God. Amen and amen! Heavenly Father, we choose to walk in the fear of the Lord, which is the beginning of wisdom. Take us further in our lessons in the School of the Spirit in receiving and retaining revelation so that we can prove all things and hold onto that which is good. We choose the Word of God to be our standard for testing the spirits to see if they be of God. Help us to walk in the wisdom ways of God concerning every expression of journaling as one of Your scribes in this hour. For Jesus Christ's sake we pray, amen and amen!

KEEP INTERPRETATION SIMPLE

Walking in a prophetic language and this amazing revelatory culture is a form of tapping into the mind and heart of God and can be an exciting and exhilarating journey. But understanding and interpreting the revelation He gives in dreams and other spiritual encounters can often be a complex and even confusing process. Therefore, let me summarize what we have discussed in a handful of concise statements that will make everything easier to remember.

1. Most of all, dreams should be interpreted on a personal basis first (John 10:3).

2. Most dreams should not be taken literally. They need interpretation (Daniel 1:17; Genesis 40:8).

3. God will use familiar terms that you know (Matthew 4:19).

4. Ponder on the dream or revelation and ask the Holy Spirit for insight (Daniel 7:8; 8:15-16; Luke 2:19; 1 Corinthians 2:12-14).

5. Ask the Holy Spirit what the central thought, word, or issue is in the revelation. Reduce the dream to its simplest form. What is the main thought?

6. Search it out in the Word. Dreams from the Lord will never go against His written Word (Proverbs 25:2).

7. What did you sense and feel from the dream? Was it a good or evil presence? What was the primary emotion?

8. Relate the dream to your circumstances and spheres of influence.

9. Consecutive dreams often have similar meanings (Genesis 41:1-7, 25-31). God will speak the same message more than once in more than one way.

10. What are the colors? Is everything black and white with one main object in color?

11. Interpretations can be on three levels: personal, church, or national and international.

12. More than one interpretation can come forth in one dream. Just as with Scripture, there is the historical context as well as the personal, present implication. So it is with dreams. It might be a general word for the church with specific applications for yourself (or others).

13. Some dreams may only be understood in the future. They unfold over time. Details will make sense down the road.

14. Write down in a journal the summary; date it; write down where you were, the time (if you woke up from it), the main emotions, and a possible interpretation.

15. The key to proper interpretation is to ask questions, questions, questions!

Finally, remember that dreams are significant to all! "There couldn't be a society of people who didn't dream. They'd be dead in two weeks."[1] To receive a dream is the human obligation that begins to move a divine purpose from the mind of God to become reality in human history.[2]

Dreams and visions are where space and time are pushed away, where God allows our inner selves to see beyond and behind the conscious plane and where possibilities and hopes, as well as all our hidden monsters, come out, come out wherever they are.

> Dreaming permits each and every one of us to be quietly and safely insane every night of our lives.[3]

But life is more than dreams. As author Mark Rutland says:

> If we idolize the primary mental image and cling to it too tenaciously, we may well despise the realization of the dream when it finally arrives. An overly cherished fantasy has the capacity to steal our joy and even blind us to the dreams for which we have longed.[4]

In closing, let us consider the cautionary wisdom of "The Preacher" in Ecclesiastes:

> *For in many dreams and in many words there is emptiness. Rather, fear God* (Ecclesiastes 5:7).

> Father, we know that dreams and visions and their interpretations belong to You. With honor coupled with a deep hunger, we ask You to give us Your wisdom applications, in Jesus' great name, amen.

Notes

1. "William S. Burroughs Quotes," Goodreads.com, accessed April 07, 2012, http://www.goodreads.com/quotes/show/55251.

2. Rutland, *Dream,* 8.

3. "William C. Dement Quotes," Goodreads.com, accessed April 07, 2012, http://www.goodreads.com/quotes/show/49000.

4. Rutland, *Dream,* 38.

SOME BASICS OF REVELATORY INTERPRETING

Now it is time to get down to some "nuts and bolts" basics of revelatory interpretation. The first principle to keep in mind is to *reduce the revelatory experience to its simplest form.* With too much detail you could miss the interpretation. That is like not seeing the forest for the trees. Keep it simple. Otherwise, you risk obscuring the meaning. Take the dream to its simplest form and build on that.

Next, remember that *context determines interpretation.* The meaning is not always the same every time. For example, a seed can mean faith, the Word, the Kingdom of God, a future harvest, etc. There are no steadfast formulas. The things of the Spirit are "spiritually discerned," not naturally discerned (1 Corinthians 2:14 NKJV).

Third, *determine whether a series of repetitious dreams is involved.* Did you have two, three, or four dreams, or are they all different aspects of the same issue? More than one dream in the same night is often just a different look or version of the same message. Joseph in the Book of Genesis had two dreams, each with different symbols, but both dreams had the same meaning. Whether it was sheaves of wheat in the field or the sun, moon, and stars in the heavens, both dreams meant that the members of Joseph's family would one day bow down to him. Joseph's dreams related to his destiny.

If you don't understand that repetitive dreams typically relate to the same subject matter, you will end up looking at them as entirely isolated dreams that have no connection to each other. In doing so you risk misinterpreting all of them. If you experience repetitive dreams, look for a common thread of meaning.

Analyze your dream by asking a series of basic questions. First, *are you observing?* Where are you in the dream? If you are in the observation mode, then the dream probably is not primarily about you. It is about someone or somewhere else. God does nothing without a witness observing issues. If you are an observer in your dream, then you are that witness. This might even mean that you are going to be a watchman or an intercessor in the situation.

Second, *are you participating?* Are you actively participating in the dream but still not the main figure? Then the dream still is not primarily about you, even though its meaning may touch you more directly than when you are merely an observer.

Third, *are you the focus?* Is everyone watching you? If you are the focus of the dream, then one of the first things you need to do is try to identify where you are. That will help you frame out the dream so all the pieces can be put into place.

Fourth, *what are the objects, thoughts, and emotions in the dream?* Are there words in the dream? What impressions and thoughts are you left with when you remember or are awakened by the dream? What is the intensity of the dream—the main emotion? You will know intuitively what the most important issues are.

INTERPRETING COLORS

Understanding the significance and use of colors is one of the key principles to proper interpretation. Colors can have both a good and positive meaning as well as an opposite bad or negative meaning.

Remember, context is the key! Dreams are full of these understandings; they are often descriptive parables of light. Let's go to *The Seer* book for some illustrations. Here are some representative examples:

1. Amber—the glory of God (Ezekiel 1:4; 8:2 KJV).

2. Black—sin, death, and famine (Lamentations 4:8; Revelation 6:5; Jeremiah 8:21).

3. Blue—Heaven, Holy Spirit (Numbers 15:38).

4. Crimson/Scarlet—blood atonement, sacrifice (Isaiah 1:18; Leviticus 14:52; Joshua 2:18,21).

5. Purple—kingship, royalty (John 19:2; Judges 8:26).

6. Red—bloodshed, war (Revelation 6:4; 12:3; 2 Kings 3:22).

7. White—purity, light, righteousness (Revelation 6:2; 7:9).

INTERPRETING NUMBERS

Like colors, numbers are highly significant both in the Bible as well as in dreams. So it is important to learn a few basic principles for interpreting numbers. If you internalize and follow the principles, they will help preserve you from interpretation error or extremes.

1. The simple numbers of 1-13 often have specific spiritual significance.

2. Multiples of these numbers, or doubling or tripling, carries basically the same meaning, only they intensify the truth.

3. The first use of the number in Scripture generally conveys its spiritual meaning (the law of first use).

4. Consistency of interpretation—God is consistent, and what a number means in Genesis is the same thing that it means through all Scripture to Revelation.

5. The spiritual significance is not always stated, but may be veiled, or hidden, or seen by comparison with other Scriptures.

6. Generally, there are good and evil, true and counterfeit, godly and satanic aspects in numbers.

Getting a little more specific, let's look at the numbers 1-13 and their possible symbolic meanings:

1. One: God, beginning, source (Genesis 1:1).

2. Two: witness, testimony (John 8:17; Matthew 18:16; Deuteronomy 17:6).

3. Three: Godhead, divine completeness (Ezekiel 14:14-18; Daniel 3:23-24).

4. Four: earth, creation, winds, seasons (Genesis 2:10; 1 Corinthians 15:39).

5. Five: Cross, grace, atonement (Gen. 1:20-23; Lev. 1:5; Ephesians 4:11).

6. Six: man, beast, satan (Gen. 1:26-31; 1 Sam. 17:4-7; Numbers 35:15).

7. Seven: perfection, completeness (Hebrews 6:1-2; Judges 14; Joshua 6).

8. Eight: new beginning (Genesis 17; 1 Peter 3:20; 2 Peter 3:8).

9. Nine: finality, fullness (Matthew 27:45; Genesis 7:1-2; Galatians 5:22-23; 1 Corinthians 12:1-12).

10. Ten: law, government (Exodus 34:28).

11. Eleven: disorganization, lawlessness, antichrist (Daniel 7:24; Genesis 32:22).

12. Twelve: defying government, apostolic fullness (Exodus 28:21; Matthew 10:2-5; Leviticus 24:5-6).

13. Thirteen: rebellion, backsliding, apostasy (Genesis 14:4; 1 Kings 11:6).

TWO OTHER FACTORS TO CONSIDER

Our revelatory experience and thus its interpretation is also affected by our culture. There are cultural and social interpretations that we must bring into our understanding as well: West versus East; North versus South; North American versus South American; European versus African; Middle Eastern versus Asian; Chinese versus Russian, etc. The degree to which you have to consider these cultural factors will depend on your sphere of influence. The larger your sphere, the more significance these cultural elements will have for you.

Another critical key to dream interpretation that is sometimes overlooked is the discipline of meditating on the Word of God:

> *When I remember You on my bed, I meditate on You in the night watches* (Psalm 63:6).

I will meditate on all Your work and muse on Your deeds (Psalm 77:12).

I will meditate on Your precepts and regard Your ways (Psalm 119:15).

I remember the days of old; I meditate on all Your doings; I muse on the work of Your hands (Psalm 143:5).

Take the time to gain understanding of the principles and metaphors of Scripture. Like the psalmist, meditate on them day and night. They can have many layers of meaning. They do with me, and by learning the ways of the Spirit, I am sure they will for you!

REVELATION IS FULL OF SYMBOLISM

reams and visions are often the language full of emotions and therefore contain much symbolism. We must learn to take our interpretations first from Scripture and then from our own lives. Throughout Scripture God is consistent with His symbolic language. The symbolism He uses in Genesis will be similar to that found in Revelation. In fact, one of the fundamental principles of biblical interpretation is the "law of first use." This simply means that how a word or image or symbol or type is used in its first appearance in Scripture is a key to how it should be interpreted throughout the Bible. This consistency in symbolic language runs true in our own lives as well.

Let me explain a little further. In the Bible, the number six often is used as a symbol for humankind. How do we know this? Refer back to the first chapter of Genesis. What happened on the sixth day of creation? Man was created. Day six is the day of man. Now let's go to the other end of the Bible, to the Book of Revelation. There we find the reference to the number 666, which is plainly identified as *"the number of a man"* (Revelation 13:18 NKJV). In the Greek there is no definite article preceding the word for "man" in this verse, so it could also be translated simply as "the number of man." The number 666 represents a false trinity, the exaltation of man—humanism being worshiped as a god. In both Genesis and Revelation, therefore, the number six is associated with humankind.

Here is another similar example. What happened on the seventh day of creation? God rested because He had finished His creative work. Therefore, the number seven is the number of rest or completion. According to the four Gospels combined, how many statements did Jesus make from the Cross? Seven. The last of these was, *"It is finished!"* (John 19:30). Jesus had finished His work; He had completed His mission. Now He could rest. Throughout the Bible the number seven is symbolically associated with rest and completion.

A similar principle applies when God speaks revelation to you. When He first introduces a word or a symbol or an image to you in a dream, you may not understand it in the beginning. But you will get it eventually, and that word, symbol, or image will become part of a pattern. Once it is introduced into your spiritual alphabet, it will become consistent in its meaning for you.

For example, let's say that you have a dream in which an apple appears and you discern through the Holy Spirit that it symbolizes Israel because Zechariah 2:8 refers to Israel as the "apple" of God's eye. Once the image of the apple has entered your spiritual alphabet as a symbol for Israel, you can be confident that whenever that image appears in a future dream, the dream has something to do with the nation of Israel. God is consistent with His revelatory symbolism.

THREE REALMS FOR INTERPRETATION OF SYMBOLS

When seeking interpretation of symbolic dream and vision language, the first place you should look always is in Scripture. The Bible is full of parables and allegories from which to draw types, shadows, and symbols. Here are some examples: the mustard seed as a metaphor for faith (see Matthew 13:31-32); incense representing the prayers of the saints (see Revelation 5:8; 8:3-4); seed as a symbol for the Word of God (see Luke 8:11); and candlesticks symbolizing the church (see Revelation 1:20). If your dream has the same symbolic image as one found in the Bible, chances are it has the same meaning.

After Scripture, a second place to look for interpretation of your revelatory symbols is in colloquial expressions that fill our memory bank. The Holy Spirit turns these into pictorial language. God takes these "sayings" and idioms and uses them to speak spiritual truth. One example of this is found in Judges 7:9-15 where a barley cake appears to Gideon in a dream. Since Gideon had spent much of his life as a thresher of wheat and barley, the barley cake was a symbol from his colloquial spiritual alphabet and had distinct meaning to him.

In the same way, God will speak to you with colloquial expressions that are familiar to you but might not be to someone else. If you are from the northern or northeastern part of the country, your colloquialisms will be different than those of someone from the Deep South, and God will speak to each of you accordingly.

The third realm for interpreting these prophetic symbols comes from our own personal revelatory alphabet. This is similar to the second realm in that the objects or symbols do not mean the same thing to you as they would to someone else. Even in the Bible the same symbol or image sometimes means something different depending on how it is used or who receives it. These exceptions, however, do *not* violate the law of first use.

God often works more than one way at a time. And sometimes the symbol or image involved has more than one facet or aspect, which allows for some variations in meaning. Context determines interpretation.

The Bible uses the image of a lamb in several different ways. In Isaiah, the Messiah is presented as a lamb led to the slaughter. John's Gospel presents Jesus as the Good Shepherd and His disciples as *little lambs.* The Book of Revelation reveals Jesus Christ the *Lamb* as a Conqueror. Spiritually speaking, all three of these images are true to a lamb's nature: it is led to the slaughter, it follows its shepherd, and it conquers in the end by walking in humility because the meek will inherit the earth.

ACTUAL VERSUS VISUAL

Insights, revelations, warnings, and prophecies from the Lord may come in supernatural *visual* dreams or in *actual* dreams.[1] *Visual* dreams are visual revelations that do not involve as much active participation on the part of the dreamer as with an actual visitation from the Lord. The dreamer simply observes and receives the message. These visual dreams may contain more symbols, mysteries, and obscurities than do other types of revelation.

Actual dreams are those in which God's tangible presence is evident in some way. To see the Lord in a dream is *visual,* but for the Lord to *manifest* Himself to you in a dream is *actual.* If you dream something angelic and sense that same presence when you wake up, it was more than just a *visual symbolic* dream. The angels were *actually* there. Quite often this will reveal itself in the form of a riveting awareness all over your body of a divine presence in the room. But if there was *no* such manifested presence when you awakened, then the dream was simply *visual,* although it may still contain a wonderful message from God.

A manifestation of blessing, healing, deliverance, or endowment of power requires an *actual* visitation from the Lord in some form. Such manifestations involve an impartation of God's anointing, which will manifest in the natural realm. Therefore, an *actual impartation* occurs and the person actively participates although his or her body is asleep.

I have vivid memories of some dream encounters that I call "the Bread of His Presence" dreams. In one of them I was carrying loaves of bread and was searching for the little mint-green blanket that belonged to our daughter Rachel. Rachel loved that blanket and for quite a few years carried it with her just about everywhere she went. In my dream, I found Rachel's blanket and wrapped the loaves of bread in it. I held them closely to my chest and noticed that the bottom of each loaf was a little satin napkin that looked like a diaper.

This was an *actual* dream because there was an *actual* presence in the room. I was asleep, but the Holy Spirit was very active. Even asleep I was talking out loud and prophesying. This was more than just a message I passively received. I declared, "Just as we parents learn to love, nurture, care for, and cherish our newborn child, so should we as believers care for, love, and cherish the bread of God's presence; then revival will come."

When I woke up, my arms were outstretched over my chest as though I was clutching those loaves of bread tightly to my chest as if they were my very own babies, wrapped in my daughter's blanket. Even as I woke I heard myself prophesying, "When we as parents will care for, love, and nourish the bread of His presence, like a parent does his newborn child, then we will have revival." In fact, I was the one who was being revived. I loved God's presence just as I had our newborn child. Though I did not see any angels in the room upon waking, the manifested presence of God was so strong you could almost cut it with a knife! Yes, let's love the bread of His presence!

Some of our experiences are full of symbolism and others...well, they are just flat-out another dimension. God shows up and shows off. When that happens, how do you write that down? With as much emotive passion as possible! God Himself still comes to visit His kids! Let it be so!

NOTE

1. For more information on this subject, see James Goll, *The Seer: The Prophetic Power of Visions, Dreams, and Open Heavens* (Shippensburg, PA: Destiny Image Publishers, Inc., 2004).

THE TWENTY MOST COMMON DREAMS

Various ministries and organizations have logged literally thousands of dreams and therefore have been able to decipher the most common dreams that people have. The following is a partial listing of these most common types of dreams. This list is not comprehensive, and the dreams are not listed in any particular order. In other words, they are not ranked by most common to least common or by any other ranking factor.

1. Dreams of Your House

This one would easily rank in the top five most common dreams. Virtually all of us have had one or more dreams in which our house appears, either the house we currently live in or one where we once lived in the past. The house normally represents your life, and the circumstances taking place in the house reflect the specific activities in your life. These dreams may also represent a church as well.

Individual rooms of the house may represent specific things. For instance, if the bedroom appears, the dream may have something to do with issues of intimacy. The bathroom may represent a need for cleansing. The family room may be a clue that God wants to work on family relationships, either your nuclear family or your church family. This is one of the most common dreams that my wife has had over the years.

2. Dreams of Going to School

These dreams often center on the taking of tests. The tests may be for the purpose of promotion. Or you might find yourself searching for your next class—an indication that guidance is needed or a graduation has just occurred. You might be repeating a class you took before, possibly meaning that you have an opportunity to learn from past failures. High school dreams may be a sign that you are enrolled in the School of the Holy Spirit (H.S.=High School=Holy Spirit). There are limitless possibilities. These are just a few examples. Interesting enough, the Teacher is always silent when giving a test!

3. Dreams of Various Vehicles

These may indicate the calling you have on your life, the vehicle of purpose that will carry you from one point to another. Cars, planes, buses, etc., may be symbols of the type or even the size of the ministry you are or will be engaged in. That's why there are different kinds of vehicles. Note the color of the vehicle. If it is a car, what is the make and model? Observe who is driving it. Are you driving or is someone else driving? If someone else is driving, who is it? Do you know the person? Is it a person from your past? If the driver is faceless, this may refer to a person who will appear sometime in your future or that the Holy Spirit Himself is your driving guide.

4. Dreams Concerning Storms

Storm dreams tend to be intercessory, spiritual warfare-type dreams. They are particularly common for people who have a calling or gift in the area of the discerning of spirits. These dreams often hint of things that are on the horizon—both dark, negative storms of demonic attack for the purpose of prayer, intercession, and spiritual warfare, as well as showers of blessing that are imminent.

5. Dreams of Flying or Soaring

Flying dreams deal with your spiritual capacity to rise above problems and difficulties and to soar into the heavenlies. These are some of the most inspirational and encouraging in tone of all dreams. When awakening from a dream where you fly or soar, you often wake up feeling exhilarated—even inebriated—in the Spirit. Ascending-type dreams are more unusual yet edifying. Remember, we are seated with Christ Jesus in the heavenly places far above all principalities and powers.

6. Dreams of Being Naked or Exposed

These dreams indicate that you will be or are becoming transparent and vulnerable. Depending on your particular situation, this may be exhilarating or fearful and could reveal feelings of shame. Note: these dreams are not meant to produce embarrassment but rather draw you into greater intimacy with the Lord and indicate places where greater transparency is required. These types of dreams often appear during times of transition where you are being dismantled in order to be re-mantled.

7. Dreams of the Condition of Your Teeth

Often, these dreams reveal the need for wisdom. Are your teeth loose, rotten, falling out, or are they bright and shiny? Do you have a good bite? Are you able to chew your cud? Teeth represent wisdom, and often teeth appear loose in a dream. What does that mean? It may mean that you need a wisdom application for something you are about to bite off. The fear of the Lord is the beginning of wisdom.

8. Dreams of Past Relationships

This kind of dream may indicate that you are being tempted to fall back into old patterns and ways of thinking. Depending upon who the person is in the dream, and what this person represents to you, these dreams might also be an indication of your need to renew your former desires and godly passions for good things in life.

Seeing a person from your past does not usually mean that you will literally renew your old relationship with that individual. Look more for what that person represents in your life—for good or bad. A person who was bad in your life may represent God's warning to you not to relapse into old habits and mindsets that were not profitable. On the other hand, a person who was good in your life may represent God's desire or intention to restore good times that you thought were gone.

9. Dreams of Dying

These dreams are not normally about the person seen in the dream in a literal sense, but are symbolic about something that is passing away or departing from your life. The type of death may be important to note. Watch, though, to see if resurrection is on the other side.

Not long ago I had a dream where I was observing my own funeral. Because I was battling cancer at the time, this dream really shook me up for a while until the Lord showed me what it really meant. I was back in my hometown in Missouri, driving a white pickup truck. My mom and dad, who are both in Heaven, were in the truck with me. I drove by our old Methodist church and saw a white hearse outside. I watched as pallbearers dressed in black brought a white casket out of the church and placed it into the hearse. Upon awakening, I realized that I was watching my own funeral.

The dream was in black and white rather than color, which was a clue to its true meaning. God was tipping me off to the enemy's desire to place a spirit of death in my thoughts. The Lord was actually strengthening me to stand against this disease as well as the spirit of death behind it. Wage war with the dreams of insight that the Lord gives to you. Fight the enemy's plans in Jesus' name! By the way, I did wage war and won the battle!

10. Dreams of Birth

Normally these dreams are not about an actual childbirth but rather about new seasons of purpose and destiny coming forth into your life. If a name is given to the child, pay close attention because that usually indicates that a new season in the purposes of God is being birthed. While I say this, there are exceptions. I remember so fondly, when my wife was pregnant with our third child, Tyler Hamilton, she had a dream that she gave birth to a little girl named Rachel. I told her that was a symbolic dream. But true to form, she was right and I was wrong—child number four came along, and her name, of course, is Rachel!

11. Dreams of Taking a Shower

These are cleansing-type dreams (toilets, showers, bathtubs, etc.) revealing things that are in the process of being flushed out of your life, cleansed and flushed away. These are good dreams, by the way. Enjoy the showers of God's love and mercy and get cleansed from the dirt of the world and its ways. Apply the blood of Jesus and get ready for a new day!

12. Dreams of Falling

These dreams may reveal a fear you have of losing control of some area of your life or, on the positive side, that you are actually becoming free of directing your own life. What substance you fall into in the dream is a major key to proper understanding. The outstanding primary emotions in these dreams will indicate which way to interpret them. Falling can be fearful, but it can also represent falling into the ocean of God's love.

13. Dreams of Chasing and Being Chased

Chasing dreams often reveal enemies that are at work, coming against your life and purpose. On the opposite side, they may indicate the passionate pursuit of God in your life, and you toward Him. Are you being chased? By whom? What emotions do you feel? Are you afraid of getting caught? Or maybe you are the one doing the chasing. Who are you chasing? Why? Again, what emotions do you feel during the chase? The answers to these questions and, particularly, the dominant emotions in the dream will often help determine the direction of its interpretation. Often the Lord appears in various forms, motioning to us, saying, "Catch Me if you can!"

14. Dreams of Relatives, Alive and Dead

Most likely, these dreams indicate generational issues at work in your life—both blessings and curses. You will need discernment as to whether to accept the blessing or cut off the darkness. This is particularly true if grandparents appear in your dreams, as they will typically indicate generational issues.

One night I had a dream in which I saw my grandfather standing on the porch of his old country house, dressed in his overalls. His white hair was shining, and he had an incredible smile on his face. To this day I am still pondering over the full meaning of this dream. My grandfather may have been a symbol for God the Father, the Ancient of Days, appearing on the front porch of our family house drawing us unto Himself.

15. Dreams Called Nightmares

Nightmares tend to be more frequent with children and new believers in Christ, just as calling dreams do. They may reveal generational enemies at work that need to be cut off. Stand against the enemies of fear. Call forth the opposite presence of the amazing love of God, which casts out fear, for fear has torment!

16. Dreams of Snakes

The snake dream is probably one of the most common of all the categories of animal dreams. These dreams reveal the serpent—the devil with his demonic hosts—at work through accusation, lying, attacks, etc. Other common dreams of this nature include dreams of spiders, bears, and even alligators. Spiders and bears are the two other major animals that appear in dreams that show fear. The spider in particular, releasing its deadly poison, is often a symbol of witchcraft and the occult.

17. Dreams of Dogs and Cats

After snakes, the most common animal to appear in dreams is the dog. A dog in your dream usually indicates friendship, loyalty, protection, and good feelings. On the other hand, dog dreams may also reveal the dark side, including growling, attacking, biting, etc. Sometimes these dreams reveal a friend who is about to betray you. Dreams with cats are also quite common. These dreams also vary in nature with everything from the feeling of being loved, to being smothered, to persnickety attitudes, the occult, and even witchcraft.

18. Dreams of Going Through Doors

These dreams generally reveal change that is coming. New ways, new opportunities, and new advancements are on the way. Similar to dreams of doors are dreams including elevators or escalators, which indicate that you are rising higher into your purpose and your calling.

19. Dreams of Clocks and Watches

Clocks or watches in a dream reveal what time it is in your life, or the need for a wake-up call in the Body of Christ or in a nation. It is time to be alert and watchful. These dreams may indicate a Scripture verse as well, giving a deeper message. Are you a watchman on the walls? If so, what watch are you on?

20. Dreams With Scripture Verses

Sometimes you may have a dream in which Bible passages appear, indicating a message from God. This phenomenon may occur in a number of ways: verbal quotes where you actually hear a voice quoting the passage, digital clock-type readouts, and dramatizations of a scene from the Bible, just to name a few. Quite often these are watchmen-type dreams, dreams of instructions filled with the ways of wisdom.

My dear Michal Ann had many encounters of this type. Her Bible was open and filled with all kinds of notes. Somewhere, somehow, she picked up on the number 111 but did not understand what it meant. When she woke up all she knew was that it somehow referred to Scripture. She searched her Bible for a little while but could not find the right passage. After asking the Holy Spirit for guidance, she fell asleep again and had a second dream. In this second dream, Mike Bickle, leader of the International House of Prayer in Kansas City, came up to her with his Bible open and said, "It is Colossians 1:11." Upon waking the second time, Michal Ann looked up the Scripture:

> [We pray] that you may be invigorated and strengthened with all power, according to the might of His glory, [to exercise] every kind of endurance and patience (perseverance and forbearance) with joy (Colossians 1:11 AMP).

That verse became a life message for Michal Ann. Why? She needed that word in her own life, and the Lord used her to give that word away, imparting it to release that nature of God in others. You can do the same! Learn your revelatory language and shift yours and other people's spiritual climates in Jesus' name!

LESSON 12

PEOPLE WHO APPEAR IN YOUR ENCOUNTERS

Another extremely common occurrence in dreams is the appearance of people—family members, friends, acquaintances, prominent leaders in church, society, or government and even complete strangers. In the majority of these cases, the people who appear in your dreams and/or visions are often symbolic in nature. Seeing a person in an encounter does not necessarily mean that you will have an encounter with that person.

There are three basic questions you can ask to help you interpret dreams in which certain people appear:

1. Who is this person in relation to you?

2. What does this person's name mean?

3. What character trait or calling does this person represent to you?

Although no list of people who appear in our dreams could ever be comprehensive, the list that follows cites the most common people or type of people whom you are likely to encounter in your dreams, along with their probable symbolism.

1. A man or woman of God in your life most probably represents a particular type of message being delivered. The important issue here is not who the person is but the message he or she bears. Focus in on the message. That is where you will most likely find the meaning behind the dream.

2. An untrustworthy person in your past may indicate a coming situation that you should not trust. Seeing someone in a dream from your past who is associated with a betrayal or a bad situation may be a warning from the Holy Spirit. These may be calls to prayer to cut off a bad situation.

3. A healing evangelist (prophetic person, etc.) appearing in your dream usually represents a healing grace that is coming your way. The identity of that healing evangelist or prophetic person is not as important as what he or she represents—the kind of ministry associated with that person.

4. A husband in your dream often means that Christ Jesus the Lord is drawing ever so close in a covenant relationship.

5. Getting married in a dream usually relates to growing intimacy with God or a new joining that is coming your way. Keep in mind, opposites attract.

6. Dreams with dead people in them speak of the common sentiment attached to those deceased loved ones. This is *not* an indication that you are "crossing over" or actually visiting this person from your past in order to receive guidance! Do not equate this with the error of seeking guidance from the spirits of the dead, as King Saul did with the spirit of Samuel

(see 1 Samuel 28:1-25). God is simply giving you a snapshot of something that the dead person represents.

7. Dreams of presidents and other people in authority are often calls to pray for national events. I used to have dreams of President Clinton where he and I were walking together and I would take his hand and suddenly be able to feel the condition of his heart. And then I would pray for him, interceding not only for his heart's condition but also for the burdens or challenges of our nation.

8. A faceless person often appears in dreams as an indication of the presence of the Holy Spirit, or possibly even angels, in your life. Sometimes people dream of a faceless man driving a bus but they don't know who he is. This, too, often represents the Holy Spirit driving the bus of your life and steering you into your life mission.

R-RATED DREAMS—AM I SICK OR WHAT?

One aspect of dreaming that many people are embarrassed to talk about, much less admit to, is the aspect of dreams that contain sexual content and/or nudity. This is an important point as many people worry that if they have such occasional dreams it automatically means they have a dirty mind, a moral problem, or some such thing. Often, however, dreams with sexual content have nothing to do literally with sexual intercourse.

The difficulty with dealing with "R-rated" dreams is illustrated by the fact that several different schools of thought exist regarding these dreams and how they should be interpreted. Generally, there are four of these. Depending on one's point of view, sexually charged dreams are:

1. A spiritual call to greater intimacy.

2. A warning of one's need of cleansing of attitudes of the mind, motives of the heart, and/or even acts of immorality.

3. A calling or a joining of union with another person or even people group.

4. Natural body dreams containing the biological and physical desires that are common to most people.

In actuality, sexual dreams cannot be confined to just any one of these four categories alone. All of them are valid at one time or another depending on the specific dream. When dealing with this kind of dream, allow for the possibility of it authentically being a body dream. It is not necessary always to spiritualize everything. Sometimes there is no spiritual content. Sometimes a dream is just a dream.

To aid you in understanding and interpreting dreams with sexual content, here are some important questions to consider:

1. Is it the same sex? Is it the opposite sex? Don't take the images at face value, particularly if same-gender sex is involved. Look for a higher meaning. For example, much of the church world breeds only after its own kind; we tend to only relate to those who are most like us. The dream may indicate a need to cross-pollinate with other members of the Body of Christ. Spiritual "inbreeding" leads to weakness and eventual extinction. Multiplication comes from sowing your seed into those who are opposite of you.

2. Is it an old love or a new love? This could indicate what you currently are passionate about. Are you being tempted to go back to something old? Is there something new on the horizon that you are becoming passionate about?

3. Does this person seem to take the place of the Lord? If so, there is a serious need for cleansing and dealing with issues of idolatry.

4. Does the dream leave you feeling dirty or clean? A dirty feeling probably means that cleansing and/or repentance of some kind are needed. Feeling clean usually points to a more positive interpretation.

5. Are you or others naked in the dream? Transparency is a good thing. But often in these dreams everyone can see what is going on in your life. These dreams are not to embarrass you but to encourage you in your vulnerability with others.

ADDITIONAL THOUGHTS ON THE SUBJECT

Dr. Joe Ibojie provides a slightly different slant in his book, *Dreams and Visions:*

> Sex in a dream suggests that you are probably making, or about to make, decisions based on a carnal nature. In Scripture, God frequently uses sexual immorality as an allegory for unfaithfulness, or deviation from spiritual truth. Frequent experience of sex in dreams speaks of carnality, but it also indicates a hidden, unbroken stronghold of lust. Rape indicates violation of the dreamer's person or integrity, and this must be averted in prayer.[1]

To further clarify the different ways that sexual dreams can be interpreted, here are some final thoughts from Joy Parrott:

> God is not a prude and He may give you some dreams that will have you sure they couldn't be from Him, yet they are.

Of course, many of these will not be divine, especially if we continue to walk in the things of this world and satisfy our fleshly desires. Yet God has recorded some risqué things in the scripture which confirms that He is not a prude. In the book of Ezekiel, God refers to Jerusalem, His people, as harlots! In Hosea, God tells the prophet Hosea to marry a prostitute as a prophetic drama of His unconditional love for His people. God told Isaiah to run around naked for three years prophesying to everything in sight! ...Such examples show that God isn't concerned about offending us or sparing our "holy ears" from hearing such things. God wants to speak to us and sometimes He will get downright blunt! He is going to speak in a language that we will understand.[2]

Understanding our dreams is one thing; interpreting them is another. In closing, however, let me leave you with a biblical promise and a thought related to understanding our dreams:

Call to Me and I will answer you, and I will tell you great and mighty things, which you do not know (Jeremiah 33:3).

Dreams do not explain the future—the future will explain the dreams. Ouch! That one stung just a bit! But just keep going on the journey with me. We will learn together as we keep on going on the road less traveled.

NOTES

1. Dr. Joe Ibojie, *Dreams and Visions: How to Receive, Interpret, and Apply Your Dreams* (San Giovanni Teatino (Ch), Italy: Destiny Image Europe, 2005), 160.

2. Joy Parrott, *Parables in the Night Seasons: Understanding Your Dreams* (Renton, WA: Glory Publications, Joy Parrott Ministries, 2002), 58-59.

TESTING
THE SPIRITS

Discernment is desperately needed in the Body of Christ. We need a clear, clean stream of prophetic grace to flow in our day. The apostle John warns believers of every age:

Beloved, do not believe every spirit, but test the spirits to see whether they are from God, because many false prophets have gone out into the world. By this you know the Spirit of God: every spirit that confesses that Jesus Christ has come in the flesh is from God; and every spirit that does not confess Jesus is not from God; this is the spirit of the antichrist, of which you have heard that it is coming, and now it is already in the world (1 John 4:1-3).

As noted earlier, we have to test the spirits because prophecy, like the other gifts of the Spirit, is delivered through imperfect people. God has chosen to deliver the prophetic to the Church through the flawed and often immature vessels of humanity. Although "inscripturated revelation" was perfect and inerrant, "prophetic revelation" in the Church of Jesus Christ does not function on this level of inspiration. This is because prophecy is not our only source or way to hear God's voice. We have the living God dwelling in our hearts and the Holy Spirit leading and guiding each of us each day. Perhaps most importantly, since Calvary, the seer and the prophet serve as a supportive and secondary role to the Bible, which is God's *"more sure Word of prophecy"* (see 2 Peter 1:19), and to the indwelling Spirit of Christ in the heart of each believer.

Another reason discernment is needed is because God has chosen to speak through many people prophetically instead of using just one or two "perfected" people in a generation. Thus there is always the possibility of mixture in the revelatory word, because He chooses to use wounded people with clay feet (see 1 Corinthians 14:29). At the same time, every believer has the basic tools to discern truth from falsehood for him or herself. The fact that revelation is open for judgment in this age proves its present, imperfect state. But remember the imperfect state of prophecy is directly linked to the imperfect state of the people who deliver it—not to an imperfect God!

Evil and deceived false prophets are not the major source of erroneous revelation to God's people today. Though this is on the rise; the vast majority of "diluted stuff" comes from sincere people who are simply adding their own insights to what started out as authentic, God-given revelation. They "add" to the nugget of God's prophetic message by drawing from things in their own human psyche, heart, emotions, concern, or sympathy. We need to learn to discern when God has stopped talking and man has continued on. Some of us over the years have called this "hamburger helper"! Whenever we share a revelation or vision that God has given us for someone else, we must be very careful to give what God has given and then clearly label or preface anything else we say as our own interpretations and views concerning that revelation or vision.

God's Word tells us that we must prove all things and hold fast to that which is good (see 1 Thessalonians 5:21). At all times we must seek the

Lord's wisdom while refusing to use "wisdom" as an excuse for fear. We must be careful not to become offended at the genuine things that the Holy Spirit is doing, no matter how strange they may appear to us. Divine revelation and visionary experiences come in many different forms, and it is vital that we understand how to discern the true from the false.

Now I know that you may be waiting for me to dish out "some of the deeper things" to you by this point. But from my perspective, I would be amiss not to make sure these foundational truths are laid well before taking us further on our "mystical journey."

With this in mind, we will glance at some "wisdom issues" in Section Four. They will help us learn how to wisely discern the various forms of revelation we will encounter in our adventure with Christ.

NINE SCRIPTURAL TESTS FOR REVELATION

N ow let's nail this down! Here is a list of nine scriptural tests by which we can test every revelation that we receive for accuracy, authority, and validity. The following truths are for all of us— whether you are an acknowledged Seer Prophet or everyday believer in the Lord Jesus Christ. Let's drop the plumb line of God's Word in our lives!

1. Does the revelation edify, exhort, or console?

> *"But one who prophesies speaks to men for **edification** and **exhortation** and **consolation**"* (1 Corinthians 14:3).

The end purpose of all true prophetic revelation is to build up, to admonish, and to encourage the people of God. Anything that is not directed to this end is not true prophecy. Jeremiah the prophet had to fulfill a negative commission, but even his difficult message contained a powerful and positive promise of God for those who were obedient (see Jeremiah 1:5,10). First Corinthians 14:26 sums it up best: *"...Let all things be done for edification."*

2. Is it in agreement with God's Word?

"All scripture is given by inspiration of God..." (2 Timothy 3:16 KJV).

True revelation always agrees with the letter and the spirit of Scripture (see 2 Corinthians 1:17-20). Where the Holy Spirit says "yea and amen" in Scripture, He also says yea and amen in revelation. He never, ever contradicts Himself.

3. Does it exalt Jesus Christ?

"He will glorify Me, for He will take of Mine and will disclose it to you" (John 16:14).

All true revelation ultimately centers on Jesus Christ and exalts and glorifies Him (see Revelation 19:10).

4. Does it have good fruit?

"Beware of the false prophets, who come to you in sheep's clothing, but inwardly are ravenous wolves. You will know them by their fruits..." (Matthew 7:15-16).

True revelatory activity produces fruit in character and conduct that agrees with the fruit of the Holy Spirit (see Ephesians 5:9; Galatians 5:22-23). Some of the aspects of character or conduct that clearly are not the fruit of the Holy Spirit include pride, arrogance, boastfulness, exaggeration, dishonesty, covetousness, financial irresponsibility, licentiousness, immorality, addictive appetites, broken marriage vows, and broken homes. Normally, any revelation that is responsible for these kinds of results is from a source other than the Holy Spirit.

5. If it predicts a future event, does it come to pass? (See Deuteronomy 18:20-22.)

Any revelation that contains a prediction concerning the future should come to pass. If it does not, then, with a few exceptions, the revelation is not from God. Exceptions may include the following issues:

a. Will of person involved.

b. National repentance—Nineveh repented, so the word did not occur.

c. Messianic predictions. (They took hundreds of years to fulfill.)

d. There is a different standard for New Testament prophets than for Old Testament prophets whose predictions played into God's Messianic plan of deliverance.

6. Does the prophetic prediction turn people toward God or away from Him? (See Deuteronomy 13:1-5.)

The fact that a person makes a prediction concerning the future that is fulfilled does not necessarily prove that person is moving by Holy Spirit-inspired revelation. If such a person, by his own ministry, turns others away from obedience to the one true God, then that person's ministry is false—even if he makes correct predictions concerning the future.

7. Does it produce liberty or bondage?

"For you have not received a spirit of slavery leading to fear again, but you have received a spirit of adoption as sons by which we cry out, 'Abba! Father!'" (Romans 8:15)

True revelation given by the Holy Spirit produces liberty, not bondage (see 1 Corinthians 14:33; 2 Timothy 1:7). The Holy Spirit never causes

God's children to act like slaves, nor does He ever motivate us by fear or legalistic compulsion.

8. Does it produce life or death?

> *"Who also made us adequate as servants of a new covenant, not of the letter but of the Spirit; for the letter kills, but the Spirit gives life"* (2 Corinthians 3:6).

True revelation from the Holy Spirit always produces life, not death.

9. Does the Holy Spirit bear witness that it is true?

> *"And as for you, the anointing which you received from Him abides in you, and you have no need for anyone to teach you; but as His anointing teaches you about all things, and is true and is not a lie, and just as it has taught you, you abide in Him"* (1 John 2:27).

The Holy Spirit within the believer always confirms true revelation from the Holy Spirit. The Holy Spirit is *"the Spirit of Truth"* (see John 16:13). He *bears witness* to that which is true, but He rejects that which is false. This ninth test is the *most subjective* test of all the tests we've presented here. For that reason, it must be used in conjunction with the previous eight objective standards.

Add these nine scriptural tests together, and you will have just dropped an anchor to keep your boat steady and safe in times of turbulence and storms. The Word of God is the anchor for our soul!

SECTION FOUR

GROWING IN STEWARDSHIP

INTRODUCTION

By wisdom a house is built, and through understanding it is established

(PROVERBS 24:3 NIV).

And Jesus grew in wisdom and stature, and in favor with God and man

(LUKE 2:52 NIV).

VISION

There is only one dependable, unshakable guide through the minefield of supernatural encounters. In a world filled with spiritual voices of the New Age and every other type and description, Christians need to know how to make their way through a spiritual field littered with hidden and deadly weapons of the enemy designed to wound or destroy the unwary and the undiscerning. It is not enough to receive and retain revelation through our process of journaling. We need to also walk in the wisdom ways of God on how to properly release the revelation the Holy Spirit has given.

Stick close to Jesus. Seek Him. Love Him! Give our all to Him. James 4:8 says it this way, *"Draw to God and He will draw near to you."* I could never overemphasize this point: Cultivate intimacy with God through a relationship with His only Son, Jesus! Yes, God still speaks today and He is very capable of preserving us from harm and deception. In fact, devotional journaling just might be the tool you need to help you draw nearer to God Himself!

In Section Four, we will backtrack for a moment and look again at some basics in closing. Why? Ultimately, you will only be as mature as the foundation you lay and maintain in your life!

God speaks today through many different avenues including visions, dreams, angelic visitations and other supernatural encounters. He speaks through His inner voice, external audible voice, by journaling, through His creation and other awesome ways and means. Yet our most important source of revelation is the *Logos* of Scripture. The only way we can accurately and safely interpret supernatural revelation of any kind is to ask God for the spirit of wisdom and understanding and to seek the counsel of the Lord, so let's press on into maturity by maintaining the foundational principles of God.

One of the first applications in journaling and learning to walk in the devotional and revelatory ways of God was by composing "Love Letters to Jesus." I would simply take out my writing instrument and paper and begin to pen from my heart my thoughts, feelings, and love for God. It was simple and yet profound. A communal flow started happening and then I pondered a thought, "I wonder if He has anything He wants to say back to me?"

I would remain quiet and stay with the heart connect a little bit longer and just begin to pen. Sure enough, after I composed my "Love Letter to Jesus," He would respond by sending to me a "Love Letter" back, and before you knew it, the flow continued into another realm of revelatory understandings concerning many different matters.

I then learned to bring that simple application into public settings where I would teach on journaling as a tool of receiving revelation. The same thing would happen! "Love Letter to Jesus" would be followed by "Love Letter from Jesus!" This would be followed by the Holy Spirit sharing any number of revelations that He heard in the council room of Heaven. It all begins with a love relationship!

A PERSONAL TOUCH

There was a time in my life when I walked in a spirit of fear of people, fear of rejection, and fear of authority. This resulted in a human-pleasing disposition. The cure was coming into greater security with my loving Father God. God is a Father and He can be trusted.

If we ask Him for the things of the Holy Spirit in the name of Jesus, He will give us the real thing, not a counterfeit. Nonetheless, there are many issues that we must consider when approaching this valuable subject of wisely testing and stewarding revelation through journaling. Let's walk in security, holding our Father's hand.

From my background, greater clarity and confidence all begins and has its ending in God's love. God's love is perfect and it has no fear in it, so learn along with me that you can trust your gracious loving Father even in all of your expressions of journaling with the Holy Spirit.

Though I am involved in many councils on regional, national and international levels and have a somewhat recognized prophetic and intercessory voice, my family and I have always been a part of a local fellowship, so what I put before you is not theory to me. It is walking in a form of simplicity and purity to Christ. We never outgrow the ABC's!

I had a clear dream some time ago where a nationally recognized leader in the Body of Christ came and stood before me and stated, "You are never too old for the Sermon on the Mount." This is my story. This is my life. I choose to align my ways with His. I choose that His ways are best and that there is safety in the House.

Points that Matter

Wisdom Principles for Journaling

1. Cultivate a humble, teachable spirit. Never allow the attitude, "God told me, and that is all there is to it." You will make mistakes. Accept that as a part of the learning process and move on.

2. Have a good working knowledge of the Bible. Remember, Rhema is based on Logos. The revelatory never conflicts with the written Word!

3. God primarily gives revelation for the area in which He has given responsibility and authority. Stay away from ego trips that motivate you to seek revelation for areas in which God has not placed you.

4. Walk together with others. Realize that until your guidance is confirmed, it should be regarded as what you think God is saying.

5. Realize that if you submit to God and resist the devil, he must flee from you! You can trust the guidance of the Holy Spirit to lead you into truth.

The Three-Stage Process

Simply put, there is the three-stage process when growing in your stewardship of the revelation:

1. Pure revelation

2. Proper interpretation

3. Wise application

Learning the Ways of Wisdom

Jesus grew in wisdom, favor and stature with God and man. For wisdom and maturity's sake, we should ask ourselves five basic questions in our quest to discern God's voice:

1. Am I regularly studying the Scriptures?

2. Am I maintaining a life of prayer?

3. Am I seeking purity, cleansing and holiness in my life?

4. Am I a worshipful member of a local Christian congregation?

5. Am I committed to a few peer relationships that can speak into my life?

Safety in the Family

God has called us to be humble servants committed to a local expression of Christ's Body, diligently studying the Scripture, praying daily, and being led by the Spirit of Truth into His purposes and individual will for our lives. We are better together. There is safety in the Father's House!

EMPOWERING PRAYER

Gracious heavenly Father, we are grateful for the lessons we have taken thus far and the wisdom we are learning. It is our aim to walk in love and yet earnestly desire the spiritual gifts. We also desire to increase in wisdom administration in how to properly steward these ways of God. Help us to receive, retain, and release words of life for our sake, for others and for our spheres of responsibility and authority. Our wonderful Father God, we love You and Your ways! Thank You for teaching us some of Your ways in this series of teachings on The Scribe. We want to be a Scribe for the King, so we set our heart and our gaze to compose "Love Letters to our Father" and believe that He will express them back to us and through us to those around us. We declare that we are growing in maturity in our capacity to receive, retain and release revelation through journaling. In Jesus' mighty name, amen and amen!

WISDOM
IN JOURNALING

Journaling is simply taking personal notes for future reference. The act of writing something down helps us retain it. Recording revelatory words in a notebook or online document helps prophetic people keep track of the unrecorded revelation they have received.

You had a dream and you have not yet figured out what it means? Write it down. Then you will not forget the details before you have had a chance to meditate on it with God's help. You had a fleeting sense that you should pray for someone and you did? Write it down. You may discover later that your sense of timing was perfect.

Your journaling will be different from mine. You may use a notebook and a pen, or your laptop. You may write down your prayers—and record God's answers as you perceive them. You may keep a record of what you sense the Holy Spirit is saying to you through His various delivery systems.

I advocate journaling as a naturally supernatural tool for retaining revelation. It is a tried and tested practice that has been used for centuries by believers; it is a fundamental and useful biblical discipline. Journaling will help you understand the revelation you receive from God. And it will help you understand your prophetic self, not to mention the One who reveals things to you.

We see plenty of biblical precedent for writing down the word of the Lord in order to keep track of it. (Actually, you could say that the Bible as a whole is something like a collection of inspired journals of various types.) God instructed Habakkuk to record his vision in writing:

> *Write down the revelation and make it plain on tablets so that a herald may run with it. For the revelation awaits an appointed time; it speaks of the end and will not prove false. Though it linger, wait for it; it will certainly come and will not delay* (Habakkuk 2:2-3 NIV).

Early in his time of exile in Babylon, Daniel received a dream and visions: *"In the first year of Belshazzar king of Babylon, Daniel had a dream, and visions passed through his mind as he was lying in bed. He wrote down the substance of his dream"* (Daniel 7:1 NIV).

When you want to write down your own dreams or visions, be careful not to get lost in the details. Write down the basic framework without spending much time trying to interpret it. That account will be enough to remind you of possibly symbolic details later.

Your journals will remind you of significant promises from God that you have received prophetically. In 2004 I was scheduled to teach a class about maturing in the prophetic at the Wagner Leadership Institute. I felt led by the Spirit to include one lesson on journaling, so in preparation I reached into the drawer in my bedroom where I kept my many journals and just pulled some of them out. At the time of the class, I simply picked out of one my journals and I randomly opened it up to read to the class as a personal example. On the page I turned to, I found a word from a dream I had recorded that I had totally forgotten about. The page read, "When you are seventy years old, the true apostolic will be in full maturation." At the time, I was fifty-two years old, and seventy seemed far in the future. In fact, I hung on to that word tightly for the next nine years as I went through cancer and many other trials; sometimes I wondered if I would even make it to the next year. As the years have rolled by, I have kept that in mind as a promise from God. Now seventy is only a few years away, and I am very much looking forward to seeing with my own eyes the apostolic in full maturation. What a promise!

An even more personal experience occurred a couple years after my dear wife passed away. I was with the Lord in prayer and He spoke these words to my spirit: "I have a surprise for you today. There is a treasure waiting for you. Look in the top drawer of Ann's nightstand." I had never opened the drawer of her nightstand.

When I opened it, I found her journals from years before, when she'd had nine straight weeks of angelic visitations. Those scribbles from when Michal Ann was visited by angels from midnight to 5:00 a.m. every night for nine straight weeks are part of my inheritance now. What a treasure! Someday I will share them with my kids as part of their legacy from their mom.

AN INVITATION TO STEP INTO THE WISDOM WAYS OF GOD

If you are called to have a prophetic ministry on any level, you will need to grow in the spirit of wisdom, to increase in wisdom as Jesus did. His heavenly wisdom is available to you simply for the asking. Start asking in faith now. I can assure you that you are in very good company as you step out and pray.

LET'S PRAY

Father, we admit that we lack wisdom, but we also declare that You are generous and that You have a vast and generous supply of wisdom for every person who calls on You. Therefore, we ask for our portion of today's wisdom. You have given each one of us various assignments today, and we cannot accomplish them at all without Your help and wisdom. We want to grow in wisdom daily, as Jesus did. We want to walk out prophetic solutions to complex problems, as Solomon did. We look forward to the increase of both wisdom and revelation that You will release to us. In the holy, great name of Jesus, Amen and amen!

PROPERLY INTERPRETING REVELATION

Some years ago I was traveling through the night by train from the Frankfurt, Germany region to Rossenheim in southern Bavaria. I was in one of the sleeping cars but, unable to sleep, I spent much of my time praying in the Spirit. The Holy Spirit kept speaking to me over and over, "Where are My Daniels? Where are My Esthers? Where are My Josephs, and where are My Deborahs?"

After many years of pondering on this word, I believe that the Holy Spirit is on a quest to find believers He can work with—believers who will dream God's dreams at any cost, have a discerning spirit to properly interpret the times, and who learn to intercede out of a posture of revelation.

Daniel, Esther, Joseph, and Deborah were godly people who possessed the spirit of revelation and who altered destinies and changed history through the revelation that was bestowed on them. They trusted the Lord for wisdom and insight and served His purposes in their generation. Today the Spirit of God is looking for like-minded and like-hearted individuals who will be the Daniels, the Esthers, the Josephs, and the Deborahs for their day.

Like the biblical heroes before them, these modern-day trailblazers will study to show themselves approved as workmen for God, rightly dividing the word of truth (revelation) that is given to them (see 2 Timothy 2:15 KJV). And, like their Old Testament counterparts, they will learn to speak the language of that revelation in a manner that is relevant to their contemporaries.

WHAT LANGUAGE DO YOU SPEAK?

Before you can interpret your dreams and visions properly or intercede effectively from the posture of revelation, you must understand the language of that revelation. In his book on dreams, Mark Rutland issues this caution:

> Believers must, of course, be cautious when seeking to understand dreams and even more prudent when acting on them. There is no substitute for wisdom and discernment in dream interpretation, and prayer is crucial to developing both. Believers should commit their subconscious minds to the Lord as well as their waking thoughts, then seek from God, in earnest prayer, understanding for the visions of the night.[1]

What language do you speak? Have you learned your spiritual alphabet? Your spiritual alphabet will be unique to you. God will speak revelation to you according to the language you speak. Doctors, nurses, and other medical and health professionals have a language all their own, a technical vocabulary that untrained laypeople cannot understand. Music has a written language that is incomprehensible to anyone who has never been taught to read the symbols. Pastors have their own language, too. This can cause problems when their language does not match that of their congregations!

What language do you speak? Whatever your language is, the Holy Spirit will speak to you in that language. Of course, I am not talking so much about languages like English, French, German, Russian, or Spanish, as I am the "language" with which we interpret life. Because each of us has different life experiences, the language by which we receive and impart revelation will be distinct to each of us. We each have a personal walk and, in a sense, a personal talk. Our spiritual alphabet, though similar, is unique to each individual.

Regardless of how our individual spiritual alphabets differ, our basic approach to interpretation should be the same. Proper interpretation can occur on many different levels. Here are three simple steps for interpreting your dream revelation:

1. Study the interpretation of words and symbols by researching their meanings as recorded in Scripture and other historical literature. Find out how biblical characters and other figures from the past interpreted these words and symbols in a dream context. This is an excellent (and probably the easiest) way to begin.

2. Develop the habit of journaling. Effective interpretation is a skill that is learned over time and with experience. Your spiritual alphabet is unique to you. Journaling will help you capture your distinct pictures, grant understanding over time, and give wisdom for your journey.

3. Welcome the anointing, gifting, and presence of the Holy Spirit. He will guide you into truth, keeping things safe yet adventurous and pure yet unreligious.

In your eagerness to reach step three, don't bypass steps one and two. Always begin with the Scriptures. Let the Bible be its own best commentary. God will never contradict His Word. Let His written Word give you insight into the meaning of His visionary revelation. Study it thoroughly.

Pray over it. Lay a solid foundation of the Word in your life to give the Holy Spirit something to breathe upon.

Interpreting dreams is like putting together a giant jigsaw puzzle with thousands of tiny pieces that must be fitted together in exactly the right order. The quickest way to complete a jigsaw puzzle is to start with the border—the framework—and the same is true with dream interpretation. Once you have the framework in place it becomes easier to see where the rest of the pieces go. Before long, the big picture begins to take shape. At least, that's the way it usually works for me. I ask the Holy Spirit to give me a thought or a word. He sheds His light on one thing, which leads me to another, and another, and then everything just starts to click.

INTERPRETATIONS BELONG TO GOD

The cardinal rule to keep in mind when properly interpreting dreams and visions is that "interpretations belong to God." He who gives you the spirit of revelation is also the one who gives you the capacity to interpret that revelation. Here are some biblical examples:

From the life of Joseph:

> *Then they said to him, "We have had a dream and there is no one to interpret it." Then Joseph said to them, "Do not interpretations belong to God? Tell it to me, please"* (Genesis 40:8).

Imagine being in the place where you are so sure that interpretations belong to God and so absolutely confident in His anointing that, like Joseph, you could say to someone, "Tell it [your dream] to me," and know that God would give you the interpretation!

From the life of Daniel:

As for these four youths, God gave them knowledge and intelligence in every branch of literature and wisdom; Daniel even understood all kinds of visions and dreams. ...As for every matter of wisdom and understanding about which the king consulted them, he found them ten times better than all the magicians and conjurers who were in all his realm (Daniel 1:17,20).

Daniel was even given the ability to interpret the handwriting on the wall that King Belshazzar saw, which foretold the king's death under God's judgment (see Daniel 5:1-31).

Although it may not come out in Aramaic or Hebrew or Greek or English or Spanish, God writes in signs to His people and He wants to give us the capacity to interpret the signs of the times. We need to pray for the Lord to release in our own day godly people of wisdom who can interpret the handwriting on the wall for our generation.

From the life of Issachar:

Of the sons of Issachar, men who understood the times, with knowledge of what Israel should do, their chiefs were two hundred; and all their kinsmen were at their command (1 Chronicles 12:32).

Two hundred chiefs "who understood the times" held an entire tribe under their command. How? People will follow a person who has revelation. People will be drawn to anyone who walks with integrity in the spirit of wisdom and revelation.

The more you learn how to listen and recognize the voice of the Spirit of God, the more He will enable you to operate on multiple levels of insight. God is the master multitasker and He can enable you to be a multitasker as well. You can listen on more than one level. You can listen to the heart of a person, you can listen to the realm of the soul, and you can listen to the

Holy Spirit. It requires a fair measure of grace and the ability to block out the noise of friction, static, and distractions, but all things are possible.

What God did before, He wants to do again! Right here, right now!

NOTE

1. Mark Rutland, *Dream* (Lake Mary, FL: Charisma House, 2003), 59.

HOW YOU ARE WIRED PROPHETICALLY

I remember walking into a conference in Minneapolis. I saw this lady up on the platform and she was painting a picture. I could tell immediately that she had received professional training, and that she had surrendered her gifts to a specialized prophetic anointing. She was "painting in the Spirit" with skill and grace. Many prophetic people are artists, poets, singers, musicians, and artisans. The Lord takes their sensitivity and training and couples it with His anointing to bring them into places where they can have real influence on the society around them for the sake of His Kingdom.

I have tried to encourage my own children in this regard. All of them are gifted artistically and as the adult children of a man who is identified as a prophet, they understood that they should not do exactly what I do. From film editing to art therapy to 3D animation to songwriting, the four of them give expression to the heart of God and influence the spheres of entertainment, the arts, media, the Church, and family.

I live in the Nashville, Tennessee area, Music City, USA. So many of the people in this city are actually called prophetically by God, but they do not understand that realm and they often mess up because they are so sensitive. They are wired in a certain way and they may never have found a safe place within the Body of Christ to be prophetic musicians. Even if you do not consider yourself a prophetic artist, you can make room for others simply by being aware of this expression of God's Spirit. I so appreciate the diversity within the Body!

Besides prophetic artists, I can identify several other prophetic categories that blend gifting and training with prophetic instincts. We have prophetic writers who express prophetic messages best in written form; in fact they are often better at writing something than they are at speaking in public. When they write, whether they pen books, articles, poems, or song lyrics, they express the heart of God to contemporary society.

We also have prophetic teachers. They are not merely prophets who happen to be asked to teach something, but teachers whose subject matter comes alive under God's anointing. The content of their teaching shines with clarity and applicability. Truly they are a valuable gift to the Body of Christ.

The anointing of a prophetic teacher may or may not overlap somewhat with that of a prophetic evangelist or a prophetic counselor. What is a prophetic evangelist? Prophetic evangelists are the ones who step out into places where they can interact with the people who have not yet responded to the Gospel message. They are not afraid of the unknown as they work (most effectively teamed up with others) to speak prophetically on the streets, retail stores, health clubs, and neighborhoods of their God-assigned localities. Often enough, signs and wonders occur as they share the love of Christ, and they can carry the Good News right into newly opened hearts.

Prophetic counselors rarely work in such a public way unless they are also teachers. Usually working one on one, prophetic counselors understand what an integrated model of wholeness looks like. They are able to combine their spiritual gifts with professional training to help bring people's hearts and minds into alignment with the love and will of God.

I believe that there are even prophetic entrepreneurs! I do not mean to imply that all entrepreneurs out there are anointed by God to initiate new ideas. But an increasing number of them are inventive people who live on the curve of discovery. Energized by the Spirit, they start new businesses, patent new inventions, and bring forth prophetic solutions to today's practical needs. They do something to benefit others with their inspired ideas.

Then there are those special people whom I call prophetic Spirit-bearers. They not only practice the presence of God in their own lives, but they also release supernatural manifestations of God's glorious presence wherever they walk. Sometimes drastic responses occur: falling in the Spirit, quaking and shaking, ecstatic speech, and more. When they show up, so do power encounters, angelic activity, and kingdom clashes. Prophetic Spirit-bearers go with the wind of the Spirit (see John 3:8). In the experience of my lifetime, one of the most effective prophetic Spirit-bearers was the late Jill Austin. She must have had special angels assigned to her, because God's fire fell wherever she ministered. She was a prophetic Spirit-bearer.

What I am trying to show is how, when a prophetic anointing saturates a blend of spiritual and natural gifts, you will see God in action—guaranteed. It makes you wonder: What kind of prophet am I and where have I been assigned? The enemy may try to keep you from grasping your call or stop you from fulfilling it, but if you cling closely to God, He will see you through.

ADMINISTERING THE PROPHETIC GIFT

There is so much to learn. Together with like-minded others, we must seek the Lord to forge ahead in our lives in the Spirit and the Word, asking Him to enable us to reflect His character and love through our words and actions.

Maturing in wisdom includes maturing in our presentation of God's word. Most of the time, the presentation of the revelation is as important as the revelation itself. There is so much to learn and to keep in mind. Here is a summary for your reference:

1. The prophetic person must learn to overcome fears and failures of the past so that they affect him less and less as he or she matures. This includes fear from past hurts, past deceptions, past corruptions and sins, and the past control of other people.

2. The prophetic person must learn to overcome his or her distinct set of hindrances to delivering trustworthy revelations. The most common hindrances fall into three

categories: (a) spirit or soul wounds, (b) preconceived opinions, and (c) legalism and argumentativeness.

3. The prophetic person must learn the value of holding his or her tongue. The practice of self-restraint exemplifies the fruit of the Spirit called patience and self-control. A good part of this restraint involves honoring authority at all times and in all places.

4. The prophetic person must never use revelation as a tool of gossip or for undermining someone destructively. The whole purpose of a gift of the Spirit is to edify, exhort, and comfort, always in love (see 1 Corinthians 14:3).

5. The prophetic person does not need to utter everything he or she knows. (A fool opens his mouth and tells all he knows, as Proverbs 29:11 says.) Learning restraint is part of learning how to keep a word until its proper time, avoiding premature release and confusion. It always means avoiding being cocky, coy, prideful, or arrogant.

6. The prophetic person learns to recognize the difference between revelation and authority, why one prophet is "heard" while another is not. The authority to be heard comes from a relational joining with God Himself along with His confirmation of a revelation through His written Word and through others. There is no room for competition or jealousy. The fruit of a delivered word must always increase faith and encourage the hearers.

7. The prophetic person learns the limits of the sphere of authority given by God. The sphere may be as small as a family or as large as international affairs, ranging from local small groups, congregations, or cities to translocal states, regions, or nations.

WISELY DISCERNING REVELATORY ENCOUNTERS

What would you think if you had a spiritual experience that made your hair stand on end? Would you write it off as absolutely satanic or "off the wall" because it didn't fit your theological code? Many people would and do. Supernatural encounters are real. The seer dimension into the spirit world is not something relegated to yesterday—it exists today and is on the rise! The question we must answer is: Do all such revelatory encounters come from the one true God or can there be other sources? How can we tell the source or nature of the spirit beings we encounter? What are the marks of a truly God-initiated encounter or revelatory experience?

There is only one dependable, unshakable guide through the minefield of supernatural encounters. In a world filled with spiritual voices of the new age and every other type and description, Christians need to know how to make their way through a spiritual field littered with hidden (and deadly) weapons of the enemy designed to wound or destroy the unwary and the undiscerning.

Entire segments of the Body of Christ have "written off" the supernatural aspects of God's Kingdom and His workings in the Church today because of fears about being deceived and led astray. Others have written it off due to excess, abuse, and the bad testimony left behind by lone rangers who are not accountable to anyone in the Body of Christ. The prophetic has been given a bad rap at times, but some of the wound has been self-inflicted. Nonetheless, God does speak to His people today and He is very capable of preserving us from harm and deception.

> [Jesus said] *For everyone who asks, receives; and he who seeks, finds; and to him who knocks, it will be opened. Now suppose one of you fathers is asked by his son for a fish; he will not give him a snake instead of a fish, will he? Or if he is asked for an egg, he will not give him a scorpion, will he? If you then, being evil, know how to give good gifts to your children, how much more will your heavenly Father give the Holy Spirit to those who ask Him?* (Luke 11:10-13)

What about it—can we trust our Father? Believe it or not, God wants us to hear His voice even more than we want to hear it! He is a gracious Father who gives good gifts to His children. What is the foundation that we must lay?

Stick close to Jesus. Seek Him. Love Him! Give our all to Him. James 4:8 says it this way: *"Draw near to God and He will draw near to you."* We could never overemphasize this point: Cultivate intimacy with God through a relationship with His only Son, Jesus Christ.

God is our Father and He can be trusted. If we ask Him for the things of the Holy Spirit in the name of Christ, He will give us the real thing, not a counterfeit. Nonetheless, there are many issues that we must consider when approaching this valuable subject of wisely judging revelatory encounters.

Some people create their own fear culture. Enough of that already! If you are a believer in the Lord Jesus Christ, you are connected to a loving

Father who does not trick His kids or give them fake stuff. He can be trusted, and trust Him we will. Ask the Father and He will give you more of the Holy Spirit!

LEARNING THE WAYS OF WISDOM

And Jesus increased in wisdom and stature, and in favor with God and men

(LUKE 2:52 NKJV).

The spirit of wisdom is one of the seven Spirits of God that I introduced to you in Chapter 9 because wisdom is one of the primary qualities of God's Holy Spirit. He is wisdom personified, and *"God has united you with Christ Jesus. For our benefit God made him to be wisdom itself"* (1 Corinthians 1:30 NLT). I would say that wisdom is even more vital to prophetic people than the divine revelation they receive, because only through God-sent wisdom can they know how to handle the word of the Lord in just the right way.

Okay, but how can we best lay hold of God's wisdom? We already know we need to surrender ourselves to His lordship and to lean on Him continually, but does that guarantee that His wisdom will flow into our lives? What should we expect? How can we recognize God's wisdom once it comes?

How does this wisdom come to us? Is it a sovereign gift from God? Is it a spiritual presence of some sort? Is our personal wisdom assembled from much reading and studying? Or does it come mostly from experience, from spending years in the School of Hard Knocks?

There is no one answer, because wisdom comes through all the above. We can see that when we simply search for the word "wisdom" in Scripture. Consider the following:

Wisdom as a gift:

> *For to one is given the word of wisdom through the Spirit, and to another the word of knowledge according to the same Spirit* (1 Corinthians 12:8).

Wisdom as a spirit:

> *The Spirit of the Lord will rest on Him, the spirit of wisdom and understanding, the spirit of counsel and strength, the spirit of knowledge and the fear of the Lord* (Isaiah 11:2).

Wisdom from studying:

> *Study to shew thyself approved unto God, a workman that needeth not to be ashamed, rightly dividing the word of truth* (2 Timothy 2:15 KJV).

Wisdom arising from life experience:

> *For a righteous man falls seven times, and rises again, but the wicked stumble in time of calamity* (Proverbs 24:16).

Even fools are thought wise when they keep silent; with their mouths shut, they seem intelligent (Proverbs 17:28 NLT).

If our dear Lord Jesus, as we see in the short passage of Scripture at the beginning of this chapter, "increased" and grew in wisdom, stature, and favor with God and men, then we should expect to do so as well. I think that is remarkable—that Jesus, who was God in the flesh, *kept increasing* in His wisdom throughout His life on earth.

Our increase in wisdom will not happen automatically, though. Like me, you surely have met people you knew many years before, perhaps when you were in high school, and you have been dismayed to see that they never matured much at all. They still act like teenagers who are "wet behind the ears," even though they may have a diploma, a career, a family, and a nice car. They do not even realize that they lack the mature wisdom that their years could have won for them.

I know that Scripture says, *the fear of the Lord is the beginning of wisdom"* (Proverbs 9:10), so humble surrender to God must be the first step. I also know we need all the wisdom we can get and that we never have enough of it as long as we are alive on this earth. The apostle James clearly stated that we must *ask* for more wisdom—and that if you do, God will grant it to you: *"If any of you lacks wisdom, let him ask of God, who gives to all generously and without reproach, and it will be given to him"* (James 1:5). Even King Solomon, who was famous for his unsurpassed wisdom, had asked God for it:

> *"So give Your servant an understanding heart to judge Your people to discern between good and evil. For who is able to judge this great people of Yours?"*
>
> *It was pleasing in the sight of the Lord that Solomon had asked this thing. God said to him, "Because you have asked this thing and have not asked for yourself long life, nor have*

asked riches for yourself, nor have you asked for the life of your enemies, but have asked for yourself discernment to understand justice, behold, I have done according to your words. Behold, I have given you a wise and discerning heart, so that there has been no one like you before you, nor shall one like you arise after you" (1 Kings 3:9-12).

How can we make our requests to God for wisdom? Well, in the simplest of terms. We simply admit, "God, I lack wisdom." And then we acknowledge, "But You have a limitless supply of wisdom and you have shown Your desire to share it with the people You have created. You have come to us as Jesus, who is wisdom itself. I ask You to release Your wisdom to me concerning the problem in front of me." And then expect God's wisdom to rise up in you. You may not have to wait long!

Ask with complete faith that God wants to answer your prayer, and He will. That is what James wrote:

But if any of you lacks wisdom, let him ask of God, who gives to all generously and without reproach, and it will be given to him. But he must ask in faith without any doubting, for the one who doubts is like the surf of the sea, driven and tossed by the wind (James 1:5-6).

WHAT IS WISDOM?

Wisdom is so important to God that altogether the words "wisdom" or "wise" are used more than four hundred and fifty-six times in the Bible. Clearly wisdom is a valuable commodity!

Yet do we even understand what wisdom is, or do we just presume we know already? Wise James again provides some idea of what God's wisdom consists of:

The wisdom that comes from heaven is first of all pure and full of quiet gentleness. Then it is peace-loving and courteous. It allows discussion and is willing to yield to others; it is full of mercy and good deeds. It is wholehearted and straightforward and sincere (James 3:17 TLB).

Synonyms for the word "wisdom" help flesh out its meaning. They include: understanding, knowledge, good sense, insight, perception, astuteness, acumen, prudence, sagacity, good judgment, and more. I want and need multiplied quantities of every one of those qualities. How about you?

Some believers in every generation exemplify wisdom to a high degree. In everything they say and do you can recognize the mind and heart of God. Their character is sterling. They care about others more than themselves. They humbly seek God before they give advice or take action. Like anybody, they can veer off the narrow way (Solomon did), but the good fruit of their lives far outweighs the bad.

Wisdom is invaluable for any believer alongside any of the gifts of the Spirit, but in this book I want to highlight its importance to the exercise of the prophetic gift. I do not need to tell you that you and I need all the wisdom we can get, particularly when we are handling a word of revelation.

SAFETY IN
THE FAMILY

L et's backtrack for a moment and re-look at some basics in closing. God still speaks today through many different avenues including visions, dreams, and angelic visitations. Another one of these ways of the Holy Spirit is called "inner knowings." We simply know that we know that we know! He also speaks to us through His inner voice, external audible voice, by journaling, through His creation and other awesome ways and means. Yet our most important source of revelation is the *Logos* canon of Scripture. The only way we can accurately and safely interpret supernatural revelation *of any kind* is to ask God for the spirit of wisdom and understanding and to seek the counsel of the Lord.

Since the Bible is our absolute standard against which we must test all spiritual experiences, it should be obvious that we need to know and study God's Word. It is our only absolute, infallible, unchanging standard of truth. Just as we must learn to crawl before we learn to walk in the natural, so we must learn the ways of the *Logos,* the written Word of God, before we can learn to safely work with *Rhema,* the revealed "now" word of God. A solid and balanced working knowledge of the New Testament is the very minimum requirement as we begin to investigate Rhema revelation in-depth. Otherwise, we have no plumb line of measurement.

God has also ordained that we find safety in our relationship to a Bible-believing fellowship. Paul wrote to the Ephesians, *"Submit yourselves one to another..."* and described many of the areas of covering that God has placed in our lives (see Ephesians 5:21 KJV). The Bible says,

"...In the multitude of counselors there is safety" (Proverbs 11:14 KJV). In an age of lawlessness, we find safety under the umbrella-like covering of the Lord, of His Word, and of the local church. We are not called to be proud religious rebels "doing our own thing." God has called us to be humble servants committed to a local expression of Christ's Body, diligently studying the Scriptures, praying daily, and being led by the Spirit of Truth into His purposes and individual will for our lives.

Though I am involved in many councils on national and international levels and have a somewhat recognized prophetic and intercessory voice, my family and I are regular members of a local Spirit-filled fellowship. So what I put before you is not theory to me. It is walking in a form of simplicity and purity to Christ. We never outgrow the ABCs! With this in mind, we should all ask ourselves five basic questions in our quest to discern God's voice in the spirit realm:

1. Am I regularly studying the Scriptures?

2. Am I maintaining a life of prayer?

3. Am I seeking purity, cleansing, and holiness in my life?

4. Am I a worshipful member of a local Christian congregation?

5. Am I committed to a few peer relationships that can speak into my life?

These building blocks must be firmly in place before we begin to investigate the principles of testing spiritual experiences. With these ABCs in place, our next step is to *"...examine everything carefully; hold fast to that which is good"* (1 Thessalonians 5:21).

Let's now put into application the principles we have learned and let's ask the Lord for an increase in revelation, interpretation, and application! Remember, He wants you to hear His voice and know His prophetic ways—more than you even want to learn them. You can rely on the Holy Spirit! He is a great teacher.

With this is in mind, let's get to it! Remember, journaling is simply another tool of The Lost Art of the Prophetic. But not anymore! It time! Let's just do it!

With a love for the ways of God!
James W. Goll

SECTION FIVE

MY PERSONAL JOURNAL—
LET'S JUST DO IT!

Your journal is a track record of your spiritual adventure,
not simply a diary to record daily activities.

Date: _____ Time: _____

Location: _____

Type of Experience: _____

Dream, Vision, or Encounter:

_____

_____

_____

_____

_____

Is there a primary Scripture to relate to this experience?

_____

_____

Are you observing, participating, or the focus?

_____

_____

What is the primary feeling contained in the experience?

_____

_____

_____

_____

Possible Interpretation:

Application and Reflection:

Write a prayer related to your revelation:

Why does God send dreams to unbelievers? Because He wants to turn their hearts toward Him! God is unwilling that anyone should perish.

Date: _____ Time: _____

Location: _____

Type of Experience: _____

Dream, Vision, or Encounter:

_____

_____

_____

_____

_____

Is there a primary Scripture to relate to this experience?

_____

_____

Are you observing, participating, or the focus?

_____

_____

What is the primary feeling contained in the experience?

_____

_____

_____

_____

Possible Interpretation:

Application and Reflection:

Write a prayer related to your revelation:

Pray for the Lord to release in our own day godly people of wisdom who can interpret the handwriting on the wall for our generation!

Date: _____ Time: _____

Location: _____

Type of Experience: _____

Dream, Vision, or Encounter:

_____
_____
_____
_____
_____

Is there a primary Scripture to relate to this experience?

_____
_____

Are you observing, participating, or the focus?

_____
_____

What is the primary feeling contained in the experience?

_____
_____
_____

Possible Interpretation:

_____
_____
_____
_____
_____
_____
_____
_____

Application and Reflection:

_____
_____
_____
_____
_____
_____
_____
_____

Write a prayer related to your revelation:

_____
_____
_____
_____
_____
_____
_____
_____

God likes playing hide and seek. We get to seek out the treasure He has hidden for us! He loves this journey of hooking us with revelation with the purpose of actually reeling us into His very heart.

Date: _____ Time: _____

Location: _____

Type of Experience: _____

Dream, Vision, or Encounter:

_____

_____

_____

_____

_____

Is there a primary Scripture to relate to this experience?

_____

_____

Are you observing, participating, or the focus?

_____

_____

What is the primary feeling contained in the experience?

_____

_____

_____

Possible Interpretation:

_____
_____
_____
_____
_____
_____
_____

Application and Reflection:

_____
_____
_____
_____
_____
_____
_____

Write a prayer related to your revelation:

_____
_____
_____
_____
_____
_____
_____

*Journaling is a tried and tested spiritual tool that will help you retain
revelation and grow in your capacity to discern the voice of
the Holy Spirit. I have tried it, and it works!*

Date: _____ Time: _____

Location: _____

Type of Experience: _____

Dream, Vision, or Encounter:

_____
_____
_____
_____
_____

Is there a primary Scripture to relate to this experience?

_____
_____

Are you observing, participating, or the focus?

_____
_____

What is the primary feeling contained in the experience?

_____
_____
_____

Possible Interpretation:

_____

_____

_____

_____

_____

_____

_____

Application and Reflection:

_____

_____

_____

_____

_____

_____

_____

Write a prayer related to your revelation:

_____

_____

_____

_____

_____

_____

_____

*"You're not disciplined enough to have a spiritual discipline.
These are spiritual privileges."*

Date: _____ Time: _____

Location: _____

Type of Experience: _____

Dream, Vision, or Encounter:

_____
_____
_____
_____
_____

Is there a primary Scripture to relate to this experience?

_____
_____

Are you observing, participating, or the focus?

_____
_____

What is the primary feeling contained in the experience?

_____
_____
_____

Possible Interpretation:

Application and Reflection:

Write a prayer related to your revelation:

*The simple art of recording revelation may prove to be one of the
missing links in your own walk of hearing God's voice.
God speaks to His children much of the time!*

Date: _____ Time: _____

Location: _____

Type of Experience: _____

Dream, Vision, or Encounter:

_____
_____
_____
_____
_____

Is there a primary Scripture to relate to this experience?

_____
_____

Are you observing, participating, or the focus?

_____
_____

What is the primary feeling contained in the experience?

_____
_____
_____

Possible Interpretation:

Application and Reflection:

Write a prayer related to your revelation:

God cares about what transpires in our lives and has made Himself available to each of us. He is not out of touch or beyond reach.

Date: _____ Time: _____

Location: _____

Type of Experience: _____

Dream, Vision, or Encounter:

_____
_____
_____
_____
_____

Is there a primary Scripture to relate to this experience?

_____
_____

Are you observing, participating, or the focus?

_____
_____

What is the primary feeling contained in the experience?

_____
_____
_____
_____

Possible Interpretation:

Application and Reflection:

Write a prayer related to your revelation:

What God did before, He wants to do again!
Right here, right now!

Date: _____ Time: _____

Location: _____

Type of Experience: _____

Dream, Vision, or Encounter:

_____
_____
_____
_____
_____

Is there a primary Scripture to relate to this experience?

_____
_____

Are you observing, participating, or the focus?

_____
_____

What is the primary feeling contained in the experience?

_____
_____
_____

Possible Interpretation:

Application and Reflection:

Write a prayer related to your revelation:

Praying, studying, fasting, worshiping—they are all
amazing spiritual privileges—with great benefits!

Date: _____ Time: _____

Location: _____

Type of Experience: _____

Dream, Vision, or Encounter:

_____
_____
_____
_____
_____

Is there a primary Scripture to relate to this experience?

_____
_____

Are you observing, participating, or the focus?

_____
_____

What is the primary feeling contained in the experience?

_____
_____
_____
_____

Possible Interpretation:

_____

_____

_____

_____

_____

_____

_____

_____

Application and Reflection:

_____

_____

_____

_____

_____

_____

_____

Write a prayer related to your revelation:

_____

_____

_____

_____

_____

_____

_____

The more you learn how to listen and recognize the voice of the Spirit of God, the more He will enable you to operate on multiple levels of insight.

Date: _____ Time: _____

Location: _____

Type of Experience: _____

Dream, Vision, or Encounter:

_____

_____

_____

_____

_____

Is there a primary Scripture to relate to this experience?

_____

_____

Are you observing, participating, or the focus?

_____

_____

What is the primary feeling contained in the experience?

_____

_____

_____

Possible Interpretation:

Application and Reflection:

Write a prayer related to your revelation:

A great revival will come and the glory of the Lord will cover the earth as the waters cover the seas. Dreams and visions are a major part of the prophetic outpouring of God's great love in the Last Days!

Date: _____ Time: _____

Location: _____

Type of Experience: _____

Dream, Vision, or Encounter:

_____
_____
_____
_____
_____

Is there a primary Scripture to relate to this experience?

_____
_____

Are you observing, participating, or the focus?

_____
_____

What is the primary feeling contained in the experience?

_____
_____
_____

Possible Interpretation:

Application and Reflection:

Write a prayer related to your revelation:

*Some of our experiences are full of symbolism and others...well,
they are just flat-out another dimension. God shows up and shows off.
When that happens, write with as much emotive passion as possible!*

Date: _____ Time: _____

Location: _____

Type of Experience: _____

Dream, Vision, or Encounter:

_____
_____
_____
_____
_____

Is there a primary Scripture to relate to this experience?

_____
_____

Are you observing, participating, or the focus?

_____
_____

What is the primary feeling contained in the experience?

_____
_____
_____

Possible Interpretation:

_____

_____

_____

_____

_____

_____

_____

Application and Reflection:

_____

_____

_____

_____

_____

_____

Write a prayer related to your revelation:

_____

_____

_____

_____

_____

_____

_____

"Where are My Daniels? Where are My Esthers?
Where are My Josephs, and where are My Deborahs?"

Date: _____ Time: _____

Location: _____

Type of Experience: _____

Dream, Vision, or Encounter:

_____
_____
_____
_____
_____

Is there a primary Scripture to relate to this experience?

_____
_____

Are you observing, participating, or the focus?

_____
_____

What is the primary feeling contained in the experience?

_____
_____
_____

Possible Interpretation:

_____

_____

_____

_____

_____

_____

_____

_____

Application and Reflection:

_____

_____

_____

_____

_____

_____

_____

Write a prayer related to your revelation:

_____

_____

_____

_____

_____

_____

_____

_____

The Holy Spirit is on a quest to find believers He can work with—believers who will dream God's dreams at any cost.

Date: _____ Time: _____

Location: _____

Type of Experience: _____

Dream, Vision, or Encounter:

_____
_____
_____
_____
_____

Is there a primary Scripture to relate to this experience?

_____
_____

Are you observing, participating, or the focus?

_____
_____

What is the primary feeling contained in the experience?

_____
_____
_____

Possible Interpretation:

_____

_____

_____

_____

_____

_____

_____

Application and Reflection:

_____

_____

_____

_____

_____

_____

_____

Write a prayer related to your revelation:

_____

_____

_____

_____

_____

_____

_____

_____

What do we do with the promises the Lord gives us?
They are worth more than any amount of money.

Date: _____ Time: _____

Location: _____

Type of Experience: _____

Dream, Vision, or Encounter:

_____

_____

_____

_____

_____

Is there a primary Scripture to relate to this experience?

_____

_____

Are you observing, participating, or the focus?

_____

_____

What is the primary feeling contained in the experience?

_____

_____

_____

Possible Interpretation:

_____
_____
_____
_____
_____
_____
_____
_____

Application and Reflection:

_____
_____
_____
_____
_____
_____
_____

Write a prayer related to your revelation:

_____
_____
_____
_____
_____
_____
_____
_____

God wants to give us the keys of revelation so that we can unlock the meanings behind our dreams. It is the glory of a king to search out a matter! Be a king, and go search it out! This is your inheritance!

Date: _____ Time: _____

Location: _____

Type of Experience: _____

Dream, Vision, or Encounter:

_____
_____
_____
_____
_____

Is there a primary Scripture to relate to this experience?

_____
_____

Are you observing, participating, or the focus?

_____
_____

What is the primary feeling contained in the experience?

_____
_____

Possible Interpretation:

_____

_____

_____

_____

_____

_____

_____

Application and Reflection:

_____

_____

_____

_____

_____

_____

_____

Write a prayer related to your revelation:

_____

_____

_____

_____

_____

_____

_____

Sometimes, God asks a question or elicits a response—not because He does not know the answer; rather, God's questions are ultimately invitations to greater intimacy with Him!

Date: _____ Time: _____

Location: _____

Type of Experience: _____

Dream, Vision, or Encounter:

_____
_____
_____
_____
_____

Is there a primary Scripture to relate to this experience?

_____
_____

Are you observing, participating, or the focus?

_____
_____

What is the primary feeling contained in the experience?

_____
_____
_____

Possible Interpretation:

Application and Reflection:

Write a prayer related to your revelation:

Before you go to sleep, toss up a simple prayer. Just declare, "Here I am, Lord; I am ready to receive." He will come; He will invade your space. Just receive!

Date: _____ Time: _____

Location: _____

Type of Experience: _____

Dream, Vision, or Encounter:

_____
_____
_____
_____
_____

Is there a primary Scripture to relate to this experience?

_____
_____

Are you observing, participating, or the focus?

_____
_____

What is the primary feeling contained in the experience?

_____
_____
_____
_____

Possible Interpretation:

_____

_____

_____

_____

_____

_____

_____

_____

Application and Reflection:

_____

_____

_____

_____

_____

_____

_____

Write a prayer related to your revelation:

_____

_____

_____

_____

_____

_____

_____

_____

Dreams do not explain the future—
the future will explain the dreams.

Date: _____ Time: _____

Location: _____

Type of Experience: _____

Dream, Vision, or Encounter:

_____
_____
_____
_____
_____

Is there a primary Scripture to relate to this experience?

_____
_____

Are you observing, participating, or the focus?

_____
_____

What is the primary feeling contained in the experience?

_____
_____
_____
_____

Possible Interpretation:

Application and Reflection:

Write a prayer related to your revelation:

I don't want to live an ordinary life and I am sure you don't either. I want to live a life in the supernatural to such an incredible degree that will cause people to say, "Behold! There is a dreamer." Let's pursue the Master Dream Weaver and His revelatory ways together!

Date: _____   Time: _____

Location: _____

Type of Experience: _____

Dream, Vision, or Encounter:

_____
_____
_____
_____

Is there a primary Scripture to relate to this experience?

_____
_____

Are you observing, participating, or the focus?

_____
_____

What is the primary feeling contained in the experience?

_____
_____
_____

Possible Interpretation:

_____
_____
_____
_____
_____
_____
_____
_____

Application and Reflection:

_____
_____
_____
_____
_____
_____
_____
_____

Write a prayer related to your revelation:

_____
_____
_____
_____
_____
_____
_____
_____

*Quietness can actually be a form of faith because it is
the opposite of anxiety and worry.*

Date: _____ Time: _____

Location: _____

Type of Experience: _____

Dream, Vision, or Encounter:

_____
_____
_____
_____
_____

Is there a primary Scripture to relate to this experience?

_____
_____

Are you observing, participating, or the focus?

_____
_____

What is the primary feeling contained in the experience?

_____
_____
_____

Possible Interpretation:

_____

_____

_____

_____

_____

_____

_____

Application and Reflection:

_____

_____

_____

_____

_____

_____

Write a prayer related to your revelation:

_____

_____

_____

_____

_____

_____

_____

What language do you speak? Whatever your language is, the Holy Spirit will speak to you in that language. We each have a personal walk and, in a sense, a personal talk. Our spiritual alphabet, though similar, is unique to each individual.

Date: _____ Time: _____

Location: _____

Type of Experience: _____

Dream, Vision, or Encounter:

_____

_____

_____

_____

Is there a primary Scripture to relate to this experience?

_____

_____

Are you observing, participating, or the focus?

_____

_____

What is the primary feeling contained in the experience?

_____

_____

_____

Possible Interpretation:

Application and Reflection:

Write a prayer related to your revelation:

Enter the Holy of Holies in your heart where Jesus the Messiah lives.
Yes, He has taken up residence within you! He is there,
and He is waiting to commune with you.

Date: _____ Time: _____

Location: _____

Type of Experience: _____

Dream, Vision, or Encounter:

_____
_____
_____
_____
_____

Is there a primary Scripture to relate to this experience?

_____
_____

Are you observing, participating, or the focus?

_____
_____

What is the primary feeling contained in the experience?

_____
_____
_____

Possible Interpretation:

_____
_____
_____
_____
_____
_____
_____
_____

Application and Reflection:

_____
_____
_____
_____
_____
_____
_____
_____

Write a prayer related to your revelation:

_____
_____
_____
_____
_____
_____
_____

The only way we can accurately and safely interpret supernatural revelation of any kind is to ask God for the spirit of wisdom and understanding and to seek the counsel of the Lord.

Date: _____ Time: _____

Location: _____

Type of Experience: _____

Dream, Vision, or Encounter:

_____

_____

_____

_____

_____

Is there a primary Scripture to relate to this experience?

_____

_____

Are you observing, participating, or the focus?

_____

_____

What is the primary feeling contained in the experience?

_____

_____

_____

Possible Interpretation:

_____
_____
_____
_____
_____
_____
_____
_____

Application and Reflection:

_____
_____
_____
_____
_____
_____
_____
_____

Write a prayer related to your revelation:

_____
_____
_____
_____
_____
_____
_____
_____

When your dreams seem to fade away, press in— because the God of dreams has not faded away. He is always there waiting to embrace you and to expand your heart's capacity to receive more of His Word, His will, and His ways. When God seems silent, press in!

Date: _____ Time: _____

Location: _____

Type of Experience: _____

Dream, Vision, or Encounter:

_____
_____
_____
_____

Is there a primary Scripture to relate to this experience?

_____
_____

Are you observing, participating, or the focus?

_____
_____

What is the primary feeling contained in the experience?

_____
_____
_____

Possible Interpretation:

_____

_____

_____

_____

_____

_____

_____

Application and Reflection:

_____

_____

_____

_____

_____

_____

Write a prayer related to your revelation:

_____

_____

_____

_____

_____

_____

_____

The Lord, the Master Dream Weaver, has a word of encouragement
for you and for all of us: "I will be your Helper!"

Date: _____ Time: _____

Location: _____

Type of Experience: _____

Dream, Vision, or Encounter:

_____

_____

_____

_____

_____

Is there a primary Scripture to relate to this experience?

_____

_____

Are you observing, participating, or the focus?

_____

_____

What is the primary feeling contained in the experience?

_____

_____

_____

Possible Interpretation:

_____

_____

_____

_____

_____

_____

_____

_____

Application and Reflection:

_____

_____

_____

_____

_____

_____

_____

Write a prayer related to your revelation:

_____

_____

_____

_____

_____

_____

_____

_____

Imagine being in the place where you are so sure that interpretations belong to God and so absolutely confident in His anointing that you could say to someone, "Tell your dream to me," and know that God would give you the interpretation!

Date: _____   Time: _____

Location: _____

Type of Experience: _____

Dream, Vision, or Encounter:

_____

_____

_____

_____

Is there a primary Scripture to relate to this experience?

_____

_____

Are you observing, participating, or the focus?

_____

_____

What is the primary feeling contained in the experience?

_____

_____

_____

Possible Interpretation:

_____
_____
_____
_____
_____
_____
_____
_____

Application and Reflection:

_____
_____
_____
_____
_____
_____
_____
_____

Write a prayer related to your revelation:

_____
_____
_____
_____
_____
_____
_____

Wage war with the dreams of insight that the Lord gives to you.
Fight the enemy's plans in Jesus' name!

Date: _____ Time: _____

Location: _____

Type of Experience: _____

Dream, Vision, or Encounter:

_____

_____

_____

_____

_____

Is there a primary Scripture to relate to this experience?

_____

_____

Are you observing, participating, or the focus?

_____

_____

What is the primary feeling contained in the experience?

_____

_____

_____

_____

Possible Interpretation:

_____

_____

_____

_____

_____

_____

_____

_____

Application and Reflection:

_____

_____

_____

_____

_____

_____

_____

Write a prayer related to your revelation:

_____

_____

_____

_____

_____

_____

_____

Often the Lord appears in various forms, motioning to us, saying,
"Catch Me if you can!"

Date: _____ Time: _____

Location: _____

Type of Experience: _____

Dream, Vision, or Encounter:

_____
_____
_____
_____
_____

Is there a primary Scripture to relate to this experience?

_____
_____

Are you observing, participating, or the focus?

_____
_____

What is the primary feeling contained in the experience?

_____
_____
_____
_____

Possible Interpretation:

_____
_____
_____
_____
_____
_____
_____
_____

Application and Reflection:

_____
_____
_____
_____
_____
_____
_____

Write a prayer related to your revelation:

_____
_____
_____
_____
_____
_____
_____
_____

Focusing the eyes of our heart upon God causes us to become inwardly still. It raises our level of faith and expectancy and results in our being more fully open to receive from God.

Date: _____ Time: _____

Location: _____

Type of Experience: _____

Dream, Vision, or Encounter:

_____

_____

_____

_____

Is there a primary Scripture to relate to this experience?

_____

_____

Are you observing, participating, or the focus?

_____

_____

What is the primary feeling contained in the experience?

_____

_____

_____

Possible Interpretation:

Application and Reflection:

Write a prayer related to your revelation:

If you seek God's face, God will
give you the spirit of understanding.

Date: _____ Time: _____

Location: _____

Type of Experience: _____

Dream, Vision, or Encounter:

_____
_____
_____
_____
_____

Is there a primary Scripture to relate to this experience?

_____
_____

Are you observing, participating, or the focus?

_____
_____

What is the primary feeling contained in the experience?

_____
_____
_____

Possible Interpretation:

_____
_____
_____
_____
_____
_____
_____
_____

Application and Reflection:

_____
_____
_____
_____
_____
_____
_____
_____

Write a prayer related to your revelation:

_____
_____
_____
_____
_____
_____
_____

Write down a summary and keep it simple! The Holy Spirit will have a way of bringing back to your remembrance the details you might need later.

Date: _____   Time: _____

Location: _____

Type of Experience: _____

Dream, Vision, or Encounter:

_____
_____
_____
_____
_____

Is there a primary Scripture to relate to this experience?

_____
_____

Are you observing, participating, or the focus?

_____
_____

What is the primary feeling contained in the experience?

_____
_____
_____
_____

Possible Interpretation:

_____
_____
_____
_____
_____
_____
_____
_____

Application and Reflection:

_____
_____
_____
_____
_____
_____
_____

Write a prayer related to your revelation:

_____
_____
_____
_____
_____
_____
_____

You were born to
be a dreamer!

Date: _____ Time: _____

Location: _____

Type of Experience: _____

Dream, Vision, or Encounter:

_____
_____
_____
_____
_____

Is there a primary Scripture to relate to this experience?

_____
_____

Are you observing, participating, or the focus?

_____
_____

What is the primary feeling contained in the experience?

_____
_____
_____

Possible Interpretation:

_____

_____

_____

_____

_____

_____

_____

Application and Reflection:

_____

_____

_____

_____

_____

_____

_____

Write a prayer related to your revelation:

_____

_____

_____

_____

_____

_____

_____

If you are a believer in the Lord Jesus Christ, you are connected to a loving Father who does not trick His kids or give them fake stuff. He can be trusted, and trust Him we will. Ask the Father and He will give you more of the Holy Spirit!

Date: _____ Time: _____

Location: _____

Type of Experience: _____

Dream, Vision, or Encounter:

_____

_____

_____

_____

Is there a primary Scripture to relate to this experience?

_____

_____

Are you observing, participating, or the focus?

_____

_____

What is the primary feeling contained in the experience?

_____

_____

_____

Possible Interpretation:

_____

_____

_____

_____

_____

_____

_____

_____

Application and Reflection:

_____

_____

_____

_____

_____

_____

_____

Write a prayer related to your revelation:

_____

_____

_____

_____

_____

_____

_____

Always put on your "mittens" of wisdom before trying to carry your cargo of revelation to its place of usefulness and purpose. Otherwise, it might spill on you!

Date: _____ Time: _____

Location: _____

Type of Experience: _____

Dream, Vision, or Encounter:

_____

_____

_____

_____

_____

Is there a primary Scripture to relate to this experience?

_____

_____

Are you observing, participating, or the focus?

_____

_____

What is the primary feeling contained in the experience?

_____

_____

_____

Possible Interpretation:

_____
_____
_____
_____
_____
_____
_____

Application and Reflection:

_____
_____
_____
_____
_____
_____
_____

Write a prayer related to your revelation:

_____
_____
_____
_____
_____
_____
_____

In becoming still, you are not trying to do anything. You simply want to be in touch with your Divine Lover, Jesus.

Date: _____ Time: _____

Location: _____

Type of Experience: _____

Dream, Vision, or Encounter:

_____

_____

_____

_____

_____

Is there a primary Scripture to relate to this experience?

_____

_____

Are you observing, participating, or the focus?

_____

_____

What is the primary feeling contained in the experience?

_____

_____

_____

Possible Interpretation:

Application and Reflection:

Write a prayer related to your revelation:

The seer dimension into the spirit world is not something relegated to yesterday—it exists today and is on the rise!

Date: _____ Time: _____

Location: _____

Type of Experience: _____

Dream, Vision, or Encounter:

_____
_____
_____
_____
_____

Is there a primary Scripture to relate to this experience?

_____
_____

Are you observing, participating, or the focus?

_____
_____

What is the primary feeling contained in the experience?

_____
_____
_____

Possible Interpretation:

_____
_____
_____
_____
_____
_____
_____
_____

Application and Reflection:

_____
_____
_____
_____
_____
_____
_____

Write a prayer related to your revelation:

_____
_____
_____
_____
_____
_____
_____

Dreams are where space and time are pushed away, where God allows our inner selves to see beyond and behind the conscious plane and where possibilities and hopes, as well as all our hidden monsters, come out, come out wherever they are.

Date: _____ Time: _____

Location: _____

Type of Experience: _____

Dream, Vision, or Encounter:

_____

_____

_____

_____

Is there a primary Scripture to relate to this experience?

_____

_____

Are you observing, participating, or the focus?

_____

_____

What is the primary feeling contained in the experience?

_____

_____

_____

Possible Interpretation:

Application and Reflection:

Write a prayer related to your revelation:

With too much detail you could miss the interpretation. That is like not seeing the forest for the trees. Keep it simple. Otherwise, you risk obscuring the meaning. Take the dream to its simplest form and build on that.

Date: _____ Time: _____

Location: _____

Type of Experience: _____

Dream, Vision, or Encounter:

_____

_____

_____

_____

_____

Is there a primary Scripture to relate to this experience?

_____

_____

Are you observing, participating, or the focus?

_____

_____

What is the primary feeling contained in the experience?

_____

_____

_____

Possible Interpretation:

_____
_____
_____
_____
_____
_____
_____
_____

Application and Reflection:

_____
_____
_____
_____
_____
_____
_____

Write a prayer related to your revelation:

_____
_____
_____
_____
_____
_____
_____

What is God's purpose in using dream language? He wants to not only spur us on to search for His message but also put us in intimate touch with the Messenger—Himself. That is His purpose—and His invitation.

Date: _____ Time: _____

Location: _____

Type of Experience: _____

Dream, Vision, or Encounter:

_____
_____
_____
_____
_____

Is there a primary Scripture to relate to this experience?

_____
_____

Are you observing, participating, or the focus?

_____
_____

What is the primary feeling contained in the experience?

_____
_____
_____

Possible Interpretation:

_____
_____
_____
_____
_____
_____
_____
_____

Application and Reflection:

_____
_____
_____
_____
_____
_____
_____

Write a prayer related to your revelation:

_____
_____
_____
_____
_____
_____
_____

You can trust the guidance of the Holy Spirit to lead you into truth.
If you submit to God and resist the devil, he must flee from you!

Date: _____ Time: _____

Location: _____

Type of Experience: _____

Dream, Vision, or Encounter:

_____
_____
_____
_____
_____

Is there a primary Scripture to relate to this experience?

_____
_____

Are you observing, participating, or the focus?

_____
_____

What is the primary feeling contained in the experience?

_____
_____
_____
_____

Possible Interpretation:

Application and Reflection:

Write a prayer related to your revelation:

You have not because you ask not!
Ask for the interpretation!

Date: _____ Time: _____

Location: _____

Type of Experience: _____

Dream, Vision, or Encounter:

_____
_____
_____
_____
_____

Is there a primary Scripture to relate to this experience?

_____
_____

Are you observing, participating, or the focus?

_____
_____

What is the primary feeling contained in the experience?

_____
_____
_____
_____

Possible Interpretation:

Application and Reflection:

Write a prayer related to your revelation:

God has an awesome plan for your life and He wants to use dream language to speak to you. He wants to place the spirit of revelation upon your life and use you to bless and build up other believers. God wants to reveal Himself, His purposes, and His ways.

Date: _____ Time: _____

Location: _____

Type of Experience: _____

Dream, Vision, or Encounter:

_____

_____

_____

_____

Is there a primary Scripture to relate to this experience?

_____

_____

Are you observing, participating, or the focus?

_____

_____

What is the primary feeling contained in the experience?

_____

_____

_____

Possible Interpretation:

_____

_____

_____

_____

_____

_____

_____

Application and Reflection:

_____

_____

_____

_____

_____

_____

_____

Write a prayer related to your revelation:

_____

_____

_____

_____

_____

_____

_____

Take the time to gain understanding of the principles and metaphors of Scripture. Like the psalmist, meditate on them day and night. They can have many layers of meaning.

Date: _____ Time: _____

Location: _____

Type of Experience: _____

Dream, Vision, or Encounter:

_____

_____

_____

_____

_____

Is there a primary Scripture to relate to this experience?

_____

_____

Are you observing, participating, or the focus?

_____

_____

What is the primary feeling contained in the experience?

_____

_____

_____

Possible Interpretation:

_____

_____

_____

_____

_____

_____

_____

_____

Application and Reflection:

_____

_____

_____

_____

_____

_____

_____

Write a prayer related to your revelation:

_____

_____

_____

_____

_____

_____

_____

_____

Dreams are indeed the supernatural communication of Heaven—love letters filled with mysteries, intrigue, and divine parables. Dream language is truly a language of the ages.

Date: _____ Time: _____

Location: _____

Type of Experience: _____

Dream, Vision, or Encounter:

_____

_____

_____

_____

_____

Is there a primary Scripture to relate to this experience?

_____

_____

Are you observing, participating, or the focus?

_____

_____

What is the primary feeling contained in the experience?

_____

_____

_____

Possible Interpretation:

_____

_____

_____

_____

_____

_____

_____

_____

Application and Reflection:

_____

_____

_____

_____

_____

_____

_____

_____

Write a prayer related to your revelation:

_____

_____

_____

_____

_____

_____

_____

_____

More than one dream in the same night is often just a different look or version of the same message. If you experience repetitive dreams, look for a common thread of meaning.

Date: _____ Time: _____

Location: _____

Type of Experience: _____

Dream, Vision, or Encounter:

_____

_____

_____

_____

_____

Is there a primary Scripture to relate to this experience?

_____

_____

Are you observing, participating, or the focus?

_____

_____

What is the primary feeling contained in the experience?

_____

_____

_____

Possible Interpretation:

_____
_____
_____
_____
_____
_____
_____
_____

Application and Reflection:

_____
_____
_____
_____
_____
_____
_____

Write a prayer related to your revelation:

_____
_____
_____
_____
_____
_____
_____
_____

The more you learn how to listen and recognize the voice of the Spirit of God, the more He will enable you to operate on multiple levels of insight. God is the master multitasker and He can enable you to be a multitasker as well!

Date: _____ Time: _____

Location: _____

Type of Experience: _____

Dream, Vision, or Encounter:

_____

_____

_____

_____

_____

Is there a primary Scripture to relate to this experience?

_____

_____

Are you observing, participating, or the focus?

_____

_____

What is the primary feeling contained in the experience?

_____

_____

_____

Possible Interpretation:

_____

_____

_____

_____

_____

_____

_____

_____

Application and Reflection:

_____

_____

_____

_____

_____

_____

_____

Write a prayer related to your revelation:

_____

_____

_____

_____

_____

_____

_____

_____

Remove external distractions so you can talk to God and listen to Him talk to you. Nothing takes the place of time alone with God!

Date: _____ Time: _____

Location: _____

Type of Experience: _____

Dream, Vision, or Encounter:

_____
_____
_____
_____
_____

Is there a primary Scripture to relate to this experience?

_____
_____

Are you observing, participating, or the focus?

_____
_____

What is the primary feeling contained in the experience?

_____
_____
_____

Possible Interpretation:

Application and Reflection:

Write a prayer related to your revelation:

When it comes to spiritual matters, we are all helpless without Him.
That is why He sent His Son Jesus to die on the Cross for our sins,
and why He sent the Holy Spirit to abide in the heart of
every believer. God loves to help the helpless!

Date: _____ Time: _____

Location: _____

Type of Experience: _____

Dream, Vision, or Encounter:

_____

_____

_____

_____

Is there a primary Scripture to relate to this experience?

_____

_____

Are you observing, participating, or the focus?

_____

_____

What is the primary feeling contained in the experience?

_____

_____

_____

Possible Interpretation:

_____

_____

_____

_____

_____

_____

_____

_____

Application and Reflection:

_____

_____

_____

_____

_____

_____

_____

Write a prayer related to your revelation:

_____

_____

_____

_____

_____

_____

_____

You can listen on more than one level. You can listen to the heart of a person, you can listen to the realm of the soul, and you can listen to the Holy Spirit. All things are possible!

Date: _____   Time: _____

Location: _____

Type of Experience: _____

Dream, Vision, or Encounter:

_____
_____
_____
_____
_____

Is there a primary Scripture to relate to this experience?

_____
_____

Are you observing, participating, or the focus?

_____
_____

What is the primary feeling contained in the experience?

_____
_____
_____

Possible Interpretation:

Application and Reflection:

Write a prayer related to your revelation:

God will speak to you with colloquial expressions that are familiar to you but might not be to someone else. God will speak to each of you accordingly.

Date: _____ Time: _____

Location: _____

Type of Experience: _____

Dream, Vision, or Encounter:

_____
_____
_____
_____
_____

Is there a primary Scripture to relate to this experience?

_____
_____

Are you observing, participating, or the focus?

_____
_____

What is the primary feeling contained in the experience?

_____
_____
_____
_____

Possible Interpretation:

_____

_____

_____

_____

_____

_____

_____

Application and Reflection:

_____

_____

_____

_____

_____

_____

_____

Write a prayer related to your revelation:

_____

_____

_____

_____

_____

_____

_____

Always begin with the Scriptures. Let the Bible be its own best commentary. God will never contradict His Word.

Date: _____ Time: _____

Location: _____

Type of Experience: _____

Dream, Vision, or Encounter:

_____
_____
_____
_____
_____

Is there a primary Scripture to relate to this experience?

_____
_____

Are you observing, participating, or the focus?

_____
_____

What is the primary feeling contained in the experience?

_____
_____
_____
_____

Possible Interpretation:

_____
_____
_____
_____
_____
_____
_____
_____

Application and Reflection:

_____
_____
_____
_____
_____
_____
_____
_____

Write a prayer related to your revelation:

_____
_____
_____
_____
_____
_____
_____
_____

"Father, we know that dreams and their interpretations belong to You. With honor coupled with a deep hunger, we ask You to give us Your wisdom applications, in Jesus' great name, Amen."

Date: _____ Time: _____

Location: _____

Type of Experience: _____

Dream, Vision, or Encounter:

_____
_____
_____
_____
_____

Is there a primary Scripture to relate to this experience?

_____
_____

Are you observing, participating, or the focus?

_____
_____

What is the primary feeling contained in the experience?

_____
_____
_____

Possible Interpretation:

_____
_____
_____
_____
_____
_____
_____
_____

Application and Reflection:

_____
_____
_____
_____
_____
_____
_____

Write a prayer related to your revelation:

_____
_____
_____
_____
_____
_____
_____
_____

All revelation is to be tested. You will make mistakes. Accept that as a part of the learning process and go on.

Date: _____ Time: _____

Location: _____

Type of Experience: _____

Dream, Vision, or Encounter:

_____
_____
_____
_____
_____

Is there a primary Scripture to relate to this experience?

_____
_____

Are you observing, participating, or the focus?

_____
_____

What is the primary feeling contained in the experience?

_____
_____
_____
_____

Possible Interpretation:

Application and Reflection:

Write a prayer related to your revelation:

God is the Master Dream Weaver. Through dreams God communicates directly with us concerning our destiny as well as the destinies of our families, our nation, and our world.

Date: _____ Time: _____

Location: _____

Type of Experience: _____

Dream, Vision, or Encounter:

_____

_____

_____

_____

_____

Is there a primary Scripture to relate to this experience?

_____

_____

Are you observing, participating, or the focus?

_____

_____

What is the primary feeling contained in the experience?

_____

_____

_____

Possible Interpretation:

_____

_____

_____

_____

_____

_____

_____

Application and Reflection:

_____

_____

_____

_____

_____

_____

Write a prayer related to your revelation:

_____

_____

_____

_____

_____

_____

_____

Center on this moment of time and experience Jesus in it. Silence the inner noise of voices, thoughts, pressures, etc., that otherwise would force their way to the top.

Date: _____ Time: _____

Location: _____

Type of Experience: _____

Dream, Vision, or Encounter:

_____

_____

_____

_____

_____

Is there a primary Scripture to relate to this experience?

_____

_____

Are you observing, participating, or the focus?

_____

_____

What is the primary feeling contained in the experience?

_____

_____

_____

Possible Interpretation:

_____

_____

_____

_____

_____

_____

_____

_____

Application and Reflection:

_____

_____

_____

_____

_____

_____

_____

Write a prayer related to your revelation:

_____

_____

_____

_____

_____

_____

_____

God wants to make you fluent once again in dream language,
the mystical language of Heaven.

Date: _____ Time: _____

Location: _____

Type of Experience: _____

Dream, Vision, or Encounter:

_____
_____
_____
_____
_____

Is there a primary Scripture to relate to this experience?

_____
_____

Are you observing, participating, or the focus?

_____
_____

What is the primary feeling contained in the experience?

_____
_____
_____

Possible Interpretation:

_____
_____
_____
_____
_____
_____
_____

Application and Reflection:

_____
_____
_____
_____
_____
_____
_____

Write a prayer related to your revelation:

_____
_____
_____
_____
_____
_____
_____

The Lord speaks mysteries, secrets, whose meaning is hidden except to those who have a heart and soul to search it out.

Date: _____ Time: _____

Location: _____

Type of Experience: _____

Dream, Vision, or Encounter:

_____
_____
_____
_____
_____

Is there a primary Scripture to relate to this experience?

_____
_____

Are you observing, participating, or the focus?

_____
_____

What is the primary feeling contained in the experience?

_____
_____
_____

Possible Interpretation:

_____
_____
_____
_____
_____
_____
_____
_____

Application and Reflection:

_____
_____
_____
_____
_____
_____
_____
_____

Write a prayer related to your revelation:

_____
_____
_____
_____
_____
_____
_____
_____

SECTION SIX

GLOSSARY OF TERMS

The following is not intended to be an official dictionary of definitions, but rather a tool to be flexibly used in the hands of believers under the leadership of the Holy Spirit. Thanks go to numerous pioneers who have blazed a trail in understanding these ways of God including Kevin Connor, Herman Riffel, John Paul Jackson, Ira Milligan, Jane Hamon, Chuck Pierce, Barbie L. Breathitt, and others who have indeed been forerunners for us all. Over time, you will grow in your interpretive grace and you will add some of your own understandings to the following dream symbols and their interpretations.

ACID: Bitter, offense, carrying a grudge, hatred, sarcasm.

ALLIGATOR: Ancient, evil out of the past (through inherited or personal sin), danger, destruction, evil spirit.

ALTAR: A symbol for sacrifice and for incense.

ANCHOR: Representation of safety and hope.

ARM: Represents God's power and strength.

ARMOR: A symbol of warfare.

ASHES: Memories, repentance, ruin, destruction.

AUTOMOBILE: Life, person, ministry.

AUTUMN: End, completion, change, repentance.

AXE: Represents warfare and judgment.

BABY: New beginning, new idea, dependent, helpless, innocent, sin.

BALANCE(S): Represents judgment.

BARN: Symbol for blessings.

BAT: Witchcraft, unstable, flighty, fear.

BEARD: Represents old age and wisdom.

BEAVER: Industrious, busy, diligent, clever, ingenious.

BED: Rest, salvation, meditation, intimacy, peace, covenant (marriage, natural or evil), self-made.

BICYCLE: Works, works of the flesh, legalism, self-righteousness, working out life's difficulties, messenger.

BIRD: Symbol of spirits, good or evil, see the parable of Jesus on the birds.

BLACK: Symbol of famine and death.

BLOOD: Symbol for sacrifice and for life (life is in the blood).

BLUE: Symbol of Heaven.

BOW: Usually represents judgment.

BREAD: Represents life.

BRICK: Represents slavery and human effort.

BRIDLE: Symbol of restraint, control.

BROTHER-IN-LAW: Partiality or adversary, fellow minister, problem relationship, partner, oneself, natural brother-in-law.

BROWN: Dead (as in plant life), repentant, born again, without spirit.

BULL: Persecution, spiritual warfare, opposition, accusation, slander, threat, economic increase.

BUTTERFLY: Freedom, flighty, fragile, temporary glory.

CAMEL: Represents servanthood, bearing the burden of others.

CANDLE: Symbol of light (Holy Spirit or the human spirit).

CANDLESTICK: Represents the Church.

CAT: Self-willed, untrainable, predator, unclean spirit, bewitching charm, stealthy, sneaky, deception, self-pity, something precious in the context of a personal pet.

CATERPILLAR: Represents judgment and destructive powers.

CENSER: Symbol of intercession and worship.

CHAIN: Symbol of binding, oppression, punishment.

CHICKEN: Fear, cowardliness; hen can be protection, gossip, motherhood; rooster can be boasting, bragging, proud; chick can be defenseless, innocent.

CIRCLE: Symbol of eternity.

CITY: Symbol of security, safety, permanency, (cities of refuge).

CLOUD and **FIERY PILLAR:** Represents Divine presence, covering and guidance.

COLT: Represents bearing burden of others or could be a portrayal of stubbornness.

CORN (Oil and Wine): Represents blessings of God.

CROW (raven): Confusion, outspoken, operating in envy or strife, hateful, direct path, unclean, God's minister of justice or provision.

CUP: Symbol of life, health, or could represent death and evil.

CYMBAL: Symbol of vibration, praise, worship.

DEER: Graceful, swift, sure-footed, agile, timid.

DESERT: Desolation, temptation, solitude.

DOG: Unbelievers, religious hypocrites.

DOOR: An opening, entrance.

DOVE: Holy Spirit.

DRAGON: Satan.

DREAMING: A message within a message, aspiration, vision.

DROWNING: Overcome, self-pity, depression, grief, sorrow, temptation, excessive debt.

DRUGS: Influence, spell, sorcery, witchcraft, control, legalism, medicine, healing.

EIGHT: New beginnings.

EIGHT-EIGHT-EIGHT: The first resurrection saints.

ELEPHANT: Invincible or thick-skinned, not easily offended, powerful, large.

ELEVATOR: Changing position, going into the spirit realm, elevated, demoted.

ELEVEN: Incompleteness, disorder.

EYE(S): Omniscience, knowledge, sight, insight, foresight.

FACE: Character, countenance.

FALLING: Unsupported, loss of support (financial, moral, public), trial, succumb, backsliding.

FATHER: Authority, God, author, originator, source, inheritance, tradition, custom, satan, natural father.

FATHER-IN-LAW: Law, authoritative relationship based on law, legalism, problem authoritative relationship, natural father-in-law.

FEATHERS: Covering, protection.

FEET: Heart, walk, way, thoughts (meditation), offense, stubborn (unmovable), rebellion (kicking), sin.

FIFTY: Symbol of liberty, freedom, Pentecost.

FIG: Relates to Israel as a nation.

FIG LEAVES: Self-atonement, self-made covering.

FINGER: Feeling, sensitivity, discernment, conviction, works, accusation (as in pointing a finger), instruction.

FIRE: Presence of God, Holiness of God, purifying, testing.

FIVE: God's grace to humans, responsibility of humanity.

FISH: Human souls.

FLIES: Evil spirits, filth of satan's kingdom. Beelzebub = "lord of flies."

FLOOD: Judgment on sin and violence (the flood from Noah's time).

FLOWER: Fading glory of humankind.

FOREST: Symbol of nations.

FORTRESS: Protection, a stronghold.

FORTY: Symbol of testing, trial, closing in victory or defeat (Israel in Wilderness and Jesus in the desert).

FORTY-TWO: Israel's oppression, the Lord's advent to the earth.

FORTY-FIVE: Preservation.

FOUNTAIN: Source of life, refreshing.

FOUR: Represents worldwide, universal (as in four corners of the earth).

FOURTEEN: Passover, time of testing.

FOX: Cunning, evil people.

FRIEND: Self, the character or circumstance of one's friend reveals something about oneself; sometimes one friend represents another (look for the same name, initials, hair color); sometimes represents actual friend.

FROG: Demons, unclean spirits.

GARDEN: Growth and fertility.

GATE: A way of entrance, power, authority.

GOLD: Kingship, kingdom glory, God or gods.

GRANDCHILD: Heir, oneself, inherited blessing or iniquity, one's spiritual legacy, actual grandchild.

GRANDPARENT: Past, spiritual inheritance (good or evil), actual grandparent.

GRAPES: Fruit of the vine, cup of the Lord.

GRASS: Frailty of the flesh.

GRASSHOPPER: Destruction.

GREEN: Prosperity, growth, life.

HAMMER: Word of God.

HAND: Symbol of strength, power, action, possession.

HARP: Praise, worship to God.

HEAD: Authority, thoughts, mind.

HEART: Emotions, motivations, desires.

HELMET: Protection for thoughts, mind.

HEN: One who gathers, protects.

HILLS: Elevation, high, loftiness.

HORN: Power, strength, defense.

HORSE: Power, strength, conquest.

HOUSE: Home, dwelling place, the Church.

INCENSE: Prayer, intercessions and worship.

JEWELS: People of God.

KEY: Authority, power to bind or loose, lock or unlock.

KISS: Agreement, covenant, enticement, betrayal, covenant breaker, deception, seduction, friend.

KNEE: Reverence, humility.

LADDER: Christ connecting Heaven and earth.

LAMB: Humility, the Church, Christ.

LEAD: Weight, wickedness, sin, burden, judgment, fool, foolishness.

LEAF: Life amid prosperity.

LEGS: Human walk, human strength.

LEOPARD: Swiftness, usually associated with vengeance.

LILIES: Beauty, majesty.

LION: Royalty and Kingship; bravery, confidence.

LIPS: Witness.

MECHANIC: Minister, Christ, prophet, pastor, counselor.

MICE: Devourer, curse, plague, timid.

MILK: Foundational truth, nourishment.

MIRROR: God's Word or one's heart, looking at oneself, looking back, memory, past, vanity.

MISCARRIAGE: Abort, failure, loss, repentance, unjust judgment.

MONEY: Power, provision, wealth, natural talents and skills, spiritual riches, power, authority, trust in human strength, covetousness.

MONKEY: Foolishness, clinging, mischief, dishonesty, addiction.

MOON: Symbol of light in darkness, sign of the Son of Man.

MOTH: Symbol of destruction.

MOTHER: Source, Church, love, kindness, spiritual or natural mother.

MOTHER-IN-LAW: Legalism, meddler, trouble, natural mother-in-law.

MOUNTAIN: Kingdoms, dignity, permanence.

MOUTH: Witness, good or evil.

NAIL: Security, establish.

NECK: Force, loveliness, or inflexibility, meekness, rebellion.

NEST: Home, place to dwell.

NET: Symbol of a catcher as in the parables, catching people.

NINE: Judgment, finality.

NINETEEN: Barren, ashamed, repentant, selflessness, without self-righteousness; faith.

NOSE: Breath, discernment.

NUDITY: Uncovered or flesh, self-justification, self-righteousness, impure, ashamed, stubborn, temptation, lust, sexual control, exhibitionism, truth, honest, nature.

OIL: Holy Spirit, anointing.

ONE: God as a unity and as a source, new beginnings.

ONE HUNDRED: Fullness, full measure, full recompense, full reward; God's election of grace, children of promise.

ONE HUNDRED NINETEEN: The resurrection day; Lord's day.

ONE HUNDRED TWENTY: End of all flesh, beginning of life in the Spirit; divine period of probation.

ONE HUNDRED FORTY-FOUR: God's ultimate in creation.

ONE HUNDRED: Revival, ingathering, final harvest of souls.

ORANGE: Danger, great jeopardy, harm; a common color combination is orange and black, which usually signifies great evil or danger; bright or fire orange can be power, force, energy.

ONE THOUSAND: Maturity, full stature, mature service, mature judgment; divine completeness and the glory of God.

OVEN: Testing, or judgment.

PALACE: Heaven, royalty.

PALM TREE: Victory, worship.

PASTURE: Places of spiritual nourishment.

PEARL: Spiritual truth.

PEN/PENCIL: Tongue, indelible words, covenant, agreement, contract, vow, publish, record, permanent, unforgettable, gossip.

PIG: Ignorance, hypocrisy, religious unbelievers, unclean people, selfish, gluttonous, vicious, vengeful.

PILLAR: Strength, steadfastness, assistance.

PINK: Flesh, sensual, immoral, moral (as in a heart of flesh); chaste, a female infant.

PIT: Prison, oppression.

PLUMB LINE: Standards of God, measuring of a life.

PLOW: Breaking new ground.

PREGNANCY: In process, sin or righteousness in process, desire, anticipation, expectancy.

PUMPKIN: Witchcraft, deception, snare, witch, trick.

PURPLE: Royalty, wealth, prosperity.

RABBIT: Increase, fast growth, multiplication; hare can be satan and his evil spirits.

RACCOON: Mischief, night raider, rascal, thief, bandit, deceitful.

RAIN: Blessing, God's Word and revival.

RAINBOW: Covenant.

RAM: Sacrifice.

RAVEN: Evil, satan.

RED: Suffering, sacrifice or sin.

RINGS: Eternity, completion.

RIVER: Revival, refreshing.

ROACH: Infestation, unclean spirits, hidden sin.

ROBE: Covering, royalty.

ROCK: Christ our rock, stability.

ROD: Rule, correction, guidance.

ROOF: Covering, oversight.

ROOT: Spiritual source, offspring.

ROPE: Binding, bondage.

ROSE: Christ and His Church.

RUBIES: Value, worth, significance.

SALT: Incorruptibility, preserve from corruption, covenant.

SAND: Similar to seed, generations.

SAPPHIRE: Beauty, value.

SCORPION: Evil spirits, evil people; pinch of pain.

SEA: Wicked nations.

SERPENT: Satan and evil spirits.

SEVEN: Completeness, perfection.

SEVENTEEN: Spiritual order, incomplete, immature, undeveloped, childish, victory.

SEVENTY: Number of increase, perfected ministry.

SHEEP: Chant, the people of God, innocent.

SHIELD: Sign of protection.

SHOE: Sign of walking, protection for your walk.

SHOULDER: Bearing the burden of another, authority, rulership.

SISTER: Spiritual sister, Church, self, natural sister.

SIX-SIX-SIX: Sign of the Mark of the Beast, antichrist.

SIXTEEN: Free-spirited, without boundaries, without law, without sin, salvation; love.

SIXTY: Pride.

SIXTY-SIX: Idol worship.

SIX HUNDRED: Warfare.

SKINS: Covering.

SMOKE: Blinding power.

SNOW: Spotlessness, radiance.

SPARROW: Small value but precious.

SPRING: New beginning, revival, fresh start, renewal, regeneration, salvation, refreshing.

STARS: Israel, generations.

STEPS: Signs of spiritual progress.

STONE: Might, permanence.

STORMS: Misfortune, difficulty, trials.

SUMMER: Harvest, opportunity, trial, heat of affliction.

SUN: Glory, brightness, light, Christ.

SWORD: Scriptures, Christ.

TEETH: Consuming power.

TEN: Law and order.

TENT: A temporary covering, not a permanent home.

TIGER: Danger, powerful minister (both good and evil).

TIN: Dross, waste, worthless, cheap, purification.

THIRTEEN: Sign of rebellion, backsliding, apostasy.

THIRTY: Maturity for ministry.

THIRTY-TWO: Covenant.

THIRTY-THREE: Promise.

THIRTY-FOUR: Naming a son.

THIRTY-FIVE: Hope.

THIRTY-SIX: Enemy.

THIRTY-SEVEN: The Word of God.

THIRTY-EIGHT: Slavery.

THIRTY-NINE: Disease.

THREE HUNDRED: Faithful remnant (Gideon's army).

TONGUE: Language, speech.

TRAIN: Continuous, unceasing work, connected, fast, Church.

TRAP: Snare, danger, trick.

TREES: Nations, individuals, the Church.

TUNNEL: Passage, transition, way of escape, troubling experience, trial, hope.

TWELVE: Divine government, apostolic government.

TWENTY-ONE: Exceeding sinfulness, of sin.

TWENTY-FOUR: Symbol of Priesthood courses and order.

TWENTY-TWO: Light.

TWENTY-THREE: Death.

TWENTY-FIVE: The forgiveness of sins.

TWENTY-SIX: The Gospel of Christ.

TWENTY-SEVEN: Preaching the Gospel.

TWENTY-EIGHT: Eternal life.

TWENTY-NINE: Departure.

TWO: Sign for witness, testimony, or unity.

TWO HUNDRED: Insufficiency.

VAN: Family (natural or Church), family ministry, fellowship.

VINE: Symbol for Israel, Christ and His Church.

VULTURE: Sign of uncleanness and devourer.

WALL: Fortification, division, refuge.

WATCH: Prophetic, intercession, being on guard.

WATERS: Nations of earth; agitation, undercurrents, crosscurrents.

WELL: Places of refreshment, source of water of life.

WHEEL: Transport, a circle, speed, spiritual activity.

WINTER: Barren, death, dormant, waiting, cold, unfriendly.

WHIRLWIND: Hurricane, sweeping power, unable to resist.

WIND: Breath of life, power of God.

WINDOW: Blessings of Heaven, openness.

WINE: Holy Spirit.

WINESKIN: Spiritual structure.

WINGS: Protection, spiritual transport.

WOLF: Satan and evil, false ministries, and teachers.

WOMAN: Church, virgin or harlot.

WOOD: Humanity.

WRESTLING: Striving, deliverance, resistance, persistence, trial, tribulation, spirit attempting to gain control.

YELLOW: Gift, marriage, family, honor, deceitful gift, timidity, fear, cowardliness.

YOKE: Servitude, slavery, or fellowship.

DIRECTIONS

EAST: Beginning: Law (therefore blessed or cursed); birth; first (Genesis 11:2; Job 38:24).

FRONT: Future or Now: As in FRONT YARD. In the presence of; prophecy; immediate; current (Genesis 6:11; Revelation 1:19).

NORTH: Spiritual: Judgment; Heaven; spiritual warfare (as in "taking your inheritance") (Proverbs 25:23; Jeremiah 1:13-14).

LEFT: Spiritual: Weakness (human), and therefore God's strength or ability; rejected. (Left Turn = spiritual change) (Judges 3:20-21; 2 Corinthians 12:9-10).

SOUTH: Natural: Sin; world; temptation; trial; flesh; corruption; deception (Joshua 10:40; Job 37:9).

RIGHT: Natural: Authority; power; the strength of man (flesh) or the power of God revealed through man; accepted. (Right Turn = natural change) (Matthew 5:29a, 30a; 1 Peter 3:22).

WEST: End: Grace; death; last; conformed (Exodus 10:19; Luke 12:54).

BACK: Past: As in BACKYARD or BACKDOOR. Previous event or experience (good or evil); what is behind (in time—for example, past sins or the sins of forefathers); unaware; unsuspecting; hidden; memory (Genesis 22:13; Joshua 8:4).

PEOPLE/RELATIVES/TRADES

BABY: New: Beginning; work; idea; the Church; sin; innocent; dependent; helpless; natural baby (1 Corinthians 3:1; Isaiah 43:19).

CARPENTER: Builder: Preacher; evangelist; laborer (good or evil); Christ (2 Kings 22:6; Isaiah 41:7).

DOCTOR: Healer: Christ; preacher; authority; medical doctor, when naturally interpreted (Mark 2:17; 2 Chronicles 16:12).

DRUNK: Influenced: Under a spell (i.e., under the influence of the Holy Spirit or a demon's spirit); controlled; fool; stubborn; rebellious; witchcraft (Ephesians 5:18; Proverbs 14:16).

EMPLOYER: Servants: Pastor, Christ; satan; actual employer, when naturally interpreted (Colossians 3:22; 2 Peter 2:19).

GIANT: Strongman: Stronghold, challenge; obstacle; trouble (Numbers 13:32-33).

INDIAN: First: Flesh (as in "the old man"); firstborn; chief; fierce; savvy; native (Colossians 3:9; Genesis 49:3).

POLICE: Authority: Natural (civil) or spiritual authority (pastors, etc.), good or evil; protection; angels or demons; an enforcer of a curse of the Law (Romans 13:1; Luke 12:11).

Vehicles and Parts

AIRPLANE: Person or work: the Church; ministry; oversight (Soaring = Moved by the Spirit). (Habakkuk 1:8; Judges 13:25).

JET: Ministry or Minister: Powerful; fast. (Passenger jet = Church; Fighter = Individual person). (Genesis 41:43; 2 Kings 10:16).

AUTOMOBILE: Life: Person; ministry (New car = New ministry or New way of life). (Genesis 41:43; 2 Kings 10:16).

AUTO WRECK: Strife: Contention; conflict, calamity; mistake or sin in ministry (as in "failure to maintain right-of-way"). (Nahum 2:4).

BICYCLE: Works: Works of the flesh (not of faith); self-righteousness; messenger. (Galatians 5:4,19).

BOAT: Church or personal ministry: (Sailboat = moved by the Spirit; Powerboat = powerful or fast progress). (Genesis 6:16; 1 Timothy 1:19).

BRAKES: Stop: Hindrance; resist; wait. (Acts 16:6-7; 2 Peter 2:14).

HELICOPTOR: Ministry: Personal; individual; the Church; versatile; stationary (when unmoving). (2 Timothy 4:2; Romans 8:14).

MOTORCYCLE: Individual: Personal ministry; independent; rebellion; selfish; pride; swift progress. (2 Peter 2:10; 1 Samuel 15:23).

PICKUP TRUCK: Work: Personal ministry or natural work. (1 Chronicles 13:7; Galatians 6:5).

REARVIEW MIRROR: Word: (Driving backward using the rearview mirror = operating by the letter of the Word instead of by God's Spirit); legalistic; looking back. (2 Corinthians 3:6; Genesis 19:26).

RAFT: Adrift: Without direction; aimless; powerless. (Ephesians 4:14).

TRACTOR: Powerful work: Slow but powerful ministry. (Acts 1:8; 4:33).

TRACTOR TRAILER: Large burden: Ministry; powerful and/or large work (truck size is often in proportion to the burden or size of the work).

MISCELLANEOUS

ANKLES: Faith: Weak ankles = weak faith; unsupported; undependable. (Ezekiel 47:3).

ARM: Strength or weakness: Savior; deliverer; helper; aid; reaching out. (Isaiah 52:10; Psalm 136:12).

BANK: Secure: Church; dependable; safe; saved; sure (as in "you can bank on it"); reserved in Heaven. (Luke 19:23; Matthew 6:20).

BINOCULARS: Insight: Understanding; prophetic vision; future event. (John 16:13; 2 Corinthians 3:13,16).

BLEEDING: Wounded: Hurt, naturally or emotionally; dying spiritually; offended; gossip; unclean. (Psalm 147:3; Proverbs 18:8).

BLOOD TRANSFUSION: Change: Regeneration; salvation; deliverance. (Titus 3:5; Romans 12:2).

BRIDGE: Faith: Trial; way; joined. (Genesis 32:22; 1 Corinthians 10:13).

BUTTER: Works: Doing (or not doing) the Word or will of God; deceptive motives; words; smooth. (Psalm 55:21; Proverbs 30:33).

CALENDAR: Time: Date: event; appointment. (Hosea 6:11).

CARDS: Facts: Honesty (as in "putting all your cards on the table"); truth; expose or reveal; dishonest; cheat; deceitful. (Romans 12:17).

CARNIVAL: Worldly: Exhibitionism; divination; competition. (Acts 16:16; Luke 21:34).

CHAIR: Position: Seat of authority; rest. (Esther 3:1; Revelation 13:2).

CHECK: Faith: The currency of the Kingdom of God; provision; trust. (Hebrews 11:1; Mark 4:40).

CHOKING: Hinder: Stumbling over something (as in "that's too much to swallow"); hatred or anger (as in "I could choke him!"). (Mark 4:19).

CHRISTMAS: Gift: Season of rejoicing; spiritual gifts; a surprise; good will. (Luke 11:13; 1 Corinthians 14:1).

CLOSET: Private: Personal, prayer; secret sin; hidden. (Matthew 6:6; Luke 8:17).

COFFEE: Bitter or Stimulant: Repentance; reaping what one has sown; desire for revenge (bitter envying). (Numbers 9:11; Job 13:26).

DITCH: Habit: Religious tradition; addition; lust; passion. (Matthew 15:14; Psalm 7:15).

DOMINOES: Continuous: Chain reaction. (Leviticus 26:37).

EARTHQUAKE: Upheaval: change (by crisis), repentance; trial; God's judgment; disaster; trauma. (Acts 16:26; Isaiah 29:6).

ECHO: Repetition: Gossip, accusation; voice of many; mocking. (Luke 23:21).

EGG: Idea: New thought; plan; promise; potential. (Luke 11:12; 1 Timothy 4:15).

FENCE: Barrier: Boundaries; obstacles; religious traditions; doctrines; inhibitions. (Genesis 11:6; Jeremiah 15:20).

GARBAGE (DUMP): Rejected: Hell; evil; vile; corruption. (Mark 9:47-48; 1 Corinthians 9:27).

GASOLINE: Fuel: Prayer, inflammatory; gossip; contention; danger. (Jude 20; Proverbs 26:20-21).

GLOVES: Covering: Protection; save; careful (as in "handle with kid gloves"). (Psalm 24:3-4; 1 Timothy 4:4-5).

MOWED GRASS: Chastisement: Sickness; financial need or distress; emotional and mental depression or anguish. (Amos 7:1-2; 1 Corinthians 11:30-32).

GRAVEYARD: Hidden: Past; curse; evil inheritance; hypocrisy; demon. (Matthew 23:27; Luke 11:44).

GRAVEL PIT: Source: The Word of God; abundant supply. (Deuteronomy 8:9; 2 Timothy 2:15).

MUDDY ROAD: Flesh: Man's way; lust; passion; temptation; difficulty caused by the weakness of the flesh. (Psalm 69:2; Isaiah 57:20).

IRONING: Correction: Change; sanctification; exhorting; teaching righteousness; God's discipline; pressure (from trials). (Ephesians 5:27).

LADDER: Ascend or Descend: Escape; enable; way; steps. (Genesis 28:12-13; John 3:13).

LIPS: Words: Seduction; speech. (Proverbs 7:21; Proverbs 10:19).

MAP: Directions: Word of God; correction; advice. (Proverbs 6:23).

MICROPHONE: Voice: Authority; ministry; influence. (Matthew 10:27).

MIRROR: Word or one's Heart: God's Word; looking back; memory, past; vanity; Moses' Law. (1 Corinthians 13:12; Proverbs 27:19).

NEWSPAPER: Announcement: Important event; public exposure; news; gossip. (Luke 8:17).

OVEN: Heart: Heat of passion; imagination; meditation; judgment. (Hosea 7:6; Psalm 21:9).

PAINTBRUSH: Covering: (house painter's brush: regeneration: remodel, renovate; love. Artist's paint brush: Illustrative; eloquent; humorous; articulate.) (1 Peter 4:8; Titus 3:5).

PARACHUTING: Leave: Bail out; escape; flee; saved. (2 Corinthians 6:17; Jeremiah 50:28).

PERFUME: Seduction: Enticement; temptation; persuasion; deception. (Proverbs 7:7,10,13; Ecclesiastes 10:1).

PIE: Whole: Business endeavors; part of the action. (Luke 12:13).

PLAY: Worship: Idolatry; covetousness; true worship; spiritual warfare; strife; competition. (Colossians 3:5; 1 Corinthians 9:24).

POSTAGE STAMP: Seal: Authority; authorization; small or seemingly insignificant, but powerful. (Esther 8:8; John 6:27).

POT/PAN/BOWL: Vessel: Doctrine; traditions; a determination or resolve; form of the truth; a person. (Romans 2:20; Jeremiah 1:13).

RADIO: Unchangeable: Unbelief; unrelenting; contentious; unceasing; tradition. (Proverbs 27:15).

RAILROAD TRACK: Tradition: Unchanging; habit; stubborn; Gospel. (Mark 7:9,13; Colossians 2:8).

RAPE: Violation: Abuse of authority; hate; desire for revenge; murder. (2 Samuel 13:12,14-15; Deuteronomy 22:25-26).

REFRIGERATOR: Heart: Motive; attitude; stored in heart; harbor. (Matthew 12:35; Mark 7:21-22).

ROCKING CHAIR: Old: Past, memories; meditation; retirement; rest. (Jeremiah 6:16).

ROLLER COASTER: Unstable: Emotional instability; unfaithfulness; wavering; manic-depressive; depression; trials; excitement. (Isaiah 40:4; James 1:6-8).

ROLLER SKATES: Speed: Fast; swift advancement or progress. (Romans 9:28).

ROUND (shape): Spiritual: (A round face, ring, building, etc.) Grace; mercy; compassion; forgiveness. (Leviticus 19:27).

SEACOAST: Boundary: Flesh (which contains and limits the human spirit); limitations; weights. (Jeremiah 5:22; 47:6-7).

SHOVEL: Tongue: Prayer; confession; slander; dig; search; inquire. (2 Kings 3:16-17; Deuteronomy 23:13).

SKIING: Faith: (Water or snow skiing) Supported by God's power through faith; fast progress. (John 6:19,21; Matthew 14:29-31).

SLEEP: Unconscious: Unaware; hidden or covered; ignorance; danger; death. (Isaiah 29:10; Romans 13:11).

SMILE: Friendly: Kindness; benevolent; without offense; seduction. (Proverbs 18:24).

SQUARE: Legalistic: (Square eyeglasses, buildings, etc.) Religious or religion; no mercy; hard or harsh; of the world. (Leviticus 19:9).

SWEEPING: Cleaning: Repentance; change; removing obstacles. (2 Corinthians 7:1,11).

SWIMMING: Spiritual: Serving God; worship; operating the gifts of the Spirit; prophecy. (Ezekiel 47:5; Ephesians 3:8).

FALSE TEETH: Replacement: Wisdom or knowledge gained through experience or previous failures; logical reasoning; tradition. (Romans 5:3-4; Colossians 2:8).

TOOTHACHE: Trial: Unfaithful; no faith; unbelief. (Tooth = Wisdom; Ache = Suffering; Broken = Potential pain, i.e. when pressure is applied.) (Proverbs 25:19).

TELEVISION: Vision: Message; prophecy; preaching; news; evil influence; wickedness. (Numbers 24:16; Daniel 2:19).

THUNDER: Change or Without Understanding: (Of what the Spirit is saying or of the signs of the times). Dispensational change (i.e., a change in the way God deals with His people); warning of impending judgment or trouble. (John 12:28-29; Psalm 18:13).

TITLE/DEED: Ownership: Authorization; possession. (Genesis 23:20).

TREE STUMP: Unbelief; roots; tenacious; obstacle; immovable; hope. (Job 14:7-9).

URINATING: Spirit: Full bladder = Pressure. Compelling urge; temptation (such as sexual lust or strife); Bladder Infection or Cancer = Offense: Enmity. (Proverbs 17:14).

WASHCLOTH: Truth: Doctrine; understanding. (Dirty cloth = False doctrine: Insincere apology; error.) (Psalm 51:7; Job 14:4).

WATERMELON: Fruit: The fruit of good or evil works; the pleasures of sin. (Seeds = Words; Water = Spirit; Sweetness = Strength; Green = Life; Red = Passion; Yellow = Gifts) (Numbers 11:5; Proverbs 1:31).

WESTERN: Frontier: ("The wild west," a western movie, etc.) Pioneer, spiritual warfare; boldness; challenge. (Deuteronomy 20:10; Joshua 3:4).

SECTION SEVEN

RECOMMENDED READING

(Many of these titles are out of print, but most are available from booksellers.)

Austin, Dorothea. *The Name Book*. Minneapolis, MN: Bethany, 1982.

Blomgren, David. *Prophetic Gatherings in the Church: The Laying on of Hands and Prophecy*. Portland, OR: Bible Temple, 1979.

——. *Song of the Lord*. Portland, OR: Bible Temple, 1978.

Breathitt, Barbie. *The Gateway to the Seer Realm*. Shippensburg, PA: Destiny Image, 2012.

——. *A-Z Dream Symbology Dictionary*. Altona, Canada: FriesenPress, 2015.

Bullinger, Ethelbert W. *Number in Scripture: Its Supernatural Design and Spiritual Significance*. Grand Rapids, MI: Kregel, 1967.

Castro, David A. *Understanding Supernatural Dreams According to the Bible*. Brooklyn, NY: Anointed Publications, 1994.

Chevreau, Guy. *Pray with Fire: Interceding in the Spirit*. Toronto: HarperPerennial/ HarperCollins, 1995.

Conner, Kevin J. *Interpreting the Symbols and Types*. Portland, OR: City Christian Publishing, 1980.

Conner, Kevin J., and Ken Malmin. *Interpreting the Scriptures*. Portland, OR: City Christian Publishing, 1983.

Crist, Terry. *Warring According to Prophecy*. New Kensington, PA: Whitaker House, 1989.

Cunningham, Loren. *Is That Really You, God?* Seattle, WA: YWAM, 1984.

Damazio, Frank. *Developing the Prophetic Ministry*. Portland, OR: Trilogy Productions, 1983.

Deere, Jack. *Surprised by the Voice of God*. Grand Rapids, MI: Zondervan Publishing House, 1996.

Edwards, Jonathan. *Life and Diary of David Brainerd.* New York: Cosimo, Inc., 2007.

Foster, Glenn. *The Purpose and Use of Prophecy.* Dubuque, IA: Kendall Hunt Publishing Co., 1988.

Frank, Anne. *Anne Frank: The Diary of a Young Girl.* New York: Bantam/ Penguin Random House, 1993.

Galloway, Jamie. *Secrets of the Seer.* Shippensburg, PA: Destiny Image, 2017.

Goll, James. *The Discerner: Hearing, Confirming, and Acting on Prophetic Revelation.* New Kensington, PA: Whitaker House, 2017.

——. *Dream Language: The Prophetic Power of Dreams, Revelations, and the Spirit of Wisdom.* Shippensburg, PA: Destiny Image, 2006.

——. *Hearing God's Voice Today: Practical Help for Listening to Him and Recognizing His Voice.* Ada, MI: Chosen Books, 2016.

——. *Praying With God's Heart: The Power and Purpose of Prophetic Intercession.* Ada, MI: Chosen Books, 2018.

——. *The Seer: The Prophetic Power of Visions, Dreams, and Open Heavens.* Shippensburg, PA: Destiny Image, 2012.

——. *The Prophet: Creating and Sustaining a Life-Giving Prophetic Culture.* Shippensburg, PA: Destiny Image, 2019.

Grudem, Wayne. *The Gift of Prophecy in the New Testament and Today.* Wheaton, IL: Crossway, 1988.

Hagin, Kenneth. *Concerning Spiritual Gifts.* Tulsa, OK: Faith Library. 1976.

——. *The Gift of Prophecy.* Tulsa, OK: Faith Library, 1982.

——. *The Holy Spirit and His Gifts.* Tulsa, OK: Faith Library , 1974.

——. *The Ministry of a Prophet.* Tulsa, OK: Faith Library, 1981.

Hamon, Bill. *Prophets and Personal Prophecy: Guidelines for Receiving, Understanding, and Fulfilling God's Personal Word to You.* Shippensburg, PA: Destiny Image, 1987.

——. *Prophets and the Prophetic Movement.* Shippensburg, PA: Destiny Image, 1990.

——. *Prophets, Pitfalls, and Principles.* Shippensburg, PA: Destiny Image, 1991.

Hamon, Jane. *Dreams and Visions.* Grand Rapids, MI: Chosen Books, 2016.

Iverson, Dick. *The Holy Spirit Today.* Portland, OR: Bible Temple, 1976.

Jacobs, Cindy. *The Voice of God.* Bloomington, MN: Chosen Books, 2016.

Joyner, Rick. *The Call.* Fort Mill, SC: Morningstar Publications, 2006.

Kelsey, Morton T. *God, Dreams, and Revelation.* Minneapolis, MN: Augsburg House, 1974.

LeClaire, Jennifer. *The Making of a Prophet.* Grand Rapids, MI: Chosen Books, 2014.

Maloney, James. *The Panoramic Seer.* Shippensburg, PA: Destiny Image, 2012.

Mumford, Bob. *Take Another Look at Guidance: Discerning the Will of God.* Plainsfield, NJ: Logos International, 1971.

Prince, Derek. *How to Judge Prophecy.* Fort Lauderdale, FL: Derek Prince, 1971.

Pytches, David. *Prophecy in the Local Church: A Practical Handbook and Historical Overview.* London: Hodder and Stoughton, 1993.

——. *Spiritual Gifts in the Local Church.* Minneapolis, MN: Bethany, 1985.

Riffel, Herman H. *Dream Interpretation: A Biblical Understanding.* Shippensburg, PA: Destiny Image, 1993.

——. *Dreams: Wisdom Within*. Shippensburg, PA: Destiny Image, 1989.

Rountree, Anna. *The Heavens Opened*. Lake Mary, FL: Charisma House, 1999.

——. *The Priestly Bride*. Lake Mary, FL: Charisma House, 2001.

Scott, Martin. *Prophecy in the Church*. Lake Mary, FL: Charisma House, 1993.

Swope, Mary Ruth. *Listening Prayer*. New Kensington, PA: Whitaker House, 1987.

Thomas, Benny. *Exploring the World of Dreams*. New Kensington, PA: Whitaker House, 1990.

Tompkins, Iverna and Judson Cornwall, *On the Ash Heap with No Answers*. Lake Mary, FL: Charisma House, 1992.

Vallotton, Kris. *Basic Training for the Prophetic Ministry*. Shippensburg, PA: Destiny Image, 2014.

Virkler, Mark and Patti. *Communion with God*. Shippensburg, PA: Destiny Image, 1990.

——. *Dialogue with God*. Gainesville, FL: Bridge-Logos, 1986.

Washington, George, Dorothy Twohig, ed. *George Washington's Diaries*. University of Virginia Press, 1999.

Werner, Ana. *The Seer's Path*. Shippensburg, PA: Destiny Image, 2017.

Wilson, Walter. *A Dictionary of Bible Types*. Grand Rapids, MI: William B. Eerdmans, 1950.

Woodworth-Etter, Maria. *A Diary of Signs & Wonders*. Tulsa, OK: Harrison House, 1980.

Yocum, Bruce. *Prophecy*. Ann Arbor, MI: Servant, 1976.

OTHER BOOKS BY JAMES W. GOLL

(Many titles feature a matching study guide
as well as audio and video presentations.)

Adventures in the Prophetic (coauthors, Michal Ann Goll, Mickey
Robinson, Patricia King, Jeff Jansen, and Ryan Wyatt)

Angelic Encounters (coauthor, Michal Ann Goll)

The Call of the Elijah Revolution (coauthor, Lou Engle)

The Coming Israel Awakening

Deliverance from Darkness

The Discerner

Discovering the Seer in You

Dream Language (coauthor, Michal Ann Goll)

Empowered Prayer

Exploring the Nature and Gift of Dreams

Fearless and Free (coauthor, Michal Ann Goll)

Exploring Your Dreams and Visions

Finding Hope

God Encounters (coauthor, Michal Ann Goll)

God Encounters Today (coauthor, Michal Ann Goll)

Hearing God's Voice Today

Intercession: The Power and Passion to Shape History

James W. Goll 365-Day Personal Prayer Guide

Kneeling on the Promises

The Lifestyle of a Prophet

The Lifestyle of a Watchman

The Lost Art of Intercession

The Lost Art of Practicing His Presence

The Lost Art of Pure Worship
(coauthor and contributors, Chris Dupré,
Jeff Deyo, Sean Feucht, Julie Meyer)

Living a Supernatural Life

Passionate Pursuit

Prayer Storm

Praying for Israel's Destiny

Praying With God's Heart

The Prophetic Intercessor

A Radical Faith

Releasing Spiritual Gifts Today

The Seer (and *The Seer Expanded*)

The Seer Devotional Journal

Shifting Shadows of Supernatural Experiences (coauthor, Julia Loren)

Strike the Mark

Women on the Frontlines series: A Call to Compassion, A Call to Courage, A Call to the Secret Place (Michal Ann Goll, with James W. Goll)

ABOUT THE AUTHOR

James W. Goll is the founder of God Encounters Ministries and numerous other ministries. He is a member of Harvest International Ministries, the Apostolic Council of Prophetic Elders, and the Bethel Leaders Network. He serves as a core instructor at Wagner University and Christian Leadership University. James is an author of more than 45 books and 20 study manuals. He is also the founder of GOLL Ideation LLC, a Life Language Coach, a recording artist, and consultant to leaders in church, business, and the arts, entertainment, and media spheres of influence.

James teaches online classes and hosts a number of webinars each year. He produces the God Encounters Today podcast along with a corresponding weekly blog. James also is the host of INSIGHT—For the Days in Which we Live, a weekly Facebook live broadcast addressing relevant subjects as a cultural commentator. God Encounters Ministries also releases free E-Blasts with audio and video messages as well.

James is an international equipper and trainer and a voice in both the global prayer and prophetic movements. He has traveled to more than fifty nations, carrying a passion for Jesus wherever he goes. His desire is to see the Body of Christ become the house of prayer for all nations and be empowered by the Holy Spirit to spread the Good News of Jesus to every country and to all peoples.

James and Michal Ann Goll were married for thirty-two years before her graduation to Heaven in the fall of 2008. James has four married adult children and a growing number of grandchildren. He makes his home in Franklin, Tennessee.

For More Information

James W. Goll

God Encounters Ministries
P.O. Box 1653
Franklin, TN 37065
Phone: 1–877–200–1604

Websites:

www.godencounters.com • www.jamesgoll.com

Emails:

info@godencounters.com • invitejames@godencounters.com

Social Media:

Follow James on

Facebook, Instagram, Twitter, XP Media, GEM Media,

Kingdom Flame, YouTube, Vimeo, Charisma Blog, and iTunes

Every believer is prophetic!

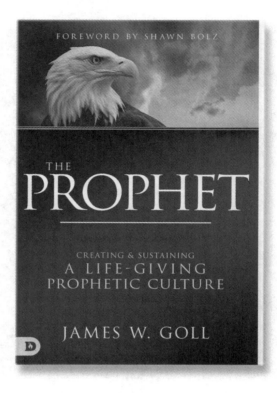

The Bible calls prophets a gift to the body of Christ. This is not because prophets hear God in our place; rather, prophets carry an impartation to connect all believers to the frequencies of Heaven with fresh clarity so they can receive and release the word of the Lord with new confidence.

James Goll is an internationally bestselling author and prophet to the nations. In this groundbreaking book, James connects you to the speaking voice of the Spirit at a greater dimension than ever before.

This comprehensive and revelatory work is broken up into four sections, focusing on Prophetic Beginnings, Development, Diversity and Commissionings.

James teaches you how to:
• Live in a realm of prophetic sensitivity
• Recognize the four levels of prophetic ministry and how they operate
• Understand the anatomy of a prophetic word
• Receive and release the gift of prophecy
•Avoid common pitfalls of prophetic ministry
• Seize your prophetic destiny
• Operate prophetically in you the sphere of influence
These words from a respected general of the prophetic movement are saturated with divine empowerment, calling forth a generation to declare words from Heaven with power, integrity and accuracy!

Satisfy the hunger in your heart!

An exciting and insightful journey into the visionary world of *The Seer*.

The prophetic movements in church history and in contemporary life are fed by two mighty streams:
• *the prophet*, whose revelation is primarily verbal.
• *the seer*, whose revelation is more visionary.

While the role of the prophet is familiar, less is known about *The Seer* dimension. To many people, these visionary prophets remain mysterious, other-worldly, and even strange. Knowledge dispels misunderstanding, and you will discover the prophetic power of dreams, visions, and life under the open heavens.

Questions answered include:
• How does visionary revelation happen? Can it be trusted?
• Where does it fit into your life and today's church?
• Can any believer become a seer? Is it a prophetic dimension reserved for the spiritually-gifted?

The Seer will move your heart and stir up your hunger for intimacy with God because the seer's goal is to reveal the person of Christ Jesus—to you, today.

Discover the prophetic power of dreams.

"...And It Is Not Because I am Wiser Than Any Living Person That I Know the Secret of Your Dream, But Because God Wanted You to Understand What You Were Thinking About" (Daniel 2:30 NLT).

After centuries of neglect, the Church is rediscovering the realm of dreams and visions as a legitimate avenue for receiving divine revelation.

Dream Language provides exciting and revealing truths about the Master Dream Weaver and His desire to communicate with you. Based on extensive biblical study and years of personal insights the authors provide in-depth examples about this fascinating realm.

You will learn how to:

* Receive and understand your dreams.
* Interpret and apply your dream revelations.
* Tune your spiritual antennae.
* Detect Dream Snatchers and Dream Drainers
* Recognize the difference between Holy Spirit, natural and demonic dreams.
* Eliminate obstacles keeping you from receiving God's revelations.

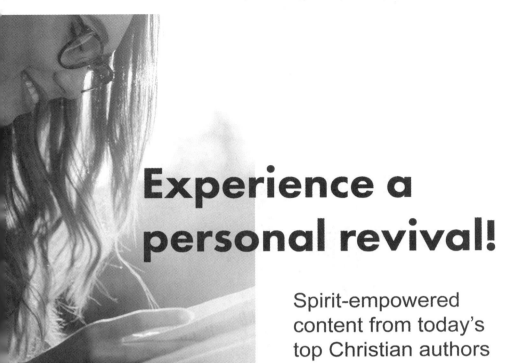